BEAUTIFUL TRAUMA

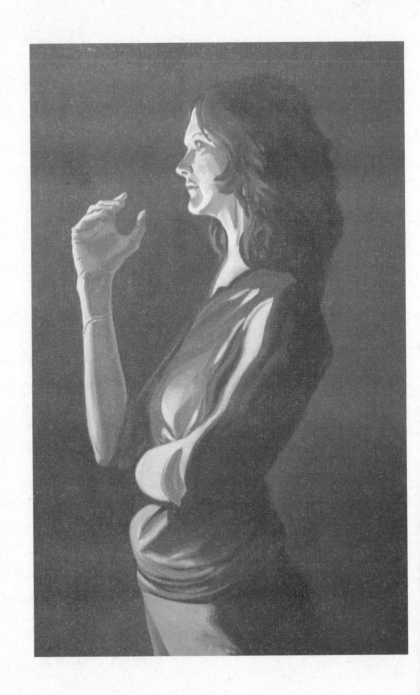

BEAUTIFUL TRAUMA

An Explosion, an Obsession,
and a New Lease on Life

REBECCA FOGG

AVERY
AN IMPRINT OF PENGUIN RANDOM HOUSE
NEW YORK

An imprint of Penguin Random House LLC
penguinrandomhouse.com

Most Avery books are available at special quantity discounts for bulk purchase for sales promotions, premiums, fund-raising, and educational needs. Special books or book excerpts also can be created to fit specific needs. For details, write SpecialMarkets@penguinrandomhouse.com.

Library of Congress Cataloging-in-Publication Data
Names: Fogg, Rebecca, author.
Title: Beautiful trauma: an explosion, an obsession, and a new lease on life / Rebecca Fogg.
Description: [New York, NY]: Avery Books, [2023] | Includes bibliographical references.
Identifiers: LCCN 2022023710 (print) | LCCN 2022023711 (ebook) | ISBN 9780593086773 (hardcover) | ISBN 9780593086780 (epub)
Subjects: LCSH: Psychic trauma—Patients—United States—Biography. | Hand—Wounds and injuries—Patients—United States—Biography. | Home accidents.
Classification: LCC RC552.T7 F64 2023 (print) | LCC RC552.T7 (ebook) | DDC 616.85/21—dc23/eng/20221013
LC record available at https://lccn.loc.gov/2022023710
LC ebook record available at https://lccn.loc.gov/2022023711

Printed in the United States of America
1st Printing

Book design by Lorie Pagnozzi
Becca's Next Life Begins Now (p. ii) copyright © Julie Unruh 2006

WITH LOVE FOR MY FAMILY, GIVEN
AND CHOSEN, ESPECIALLY ERICA,
CHARLES, AND JEN

CONTENTS

AUTHOR'S NOTE

In 2006, my right hand was partially amputated in a bizarre accident, requiring extensive repair and rehabilitation. The following is an account of how I coped with the experience by studying the science behind it, and accepting love and help, in many forms, from many people. Chapter content alternates between chronological memoir and science (anatomy, neuroscience, psychology, and then some), and in the happy event that the latter whets your appetite for more, I have included a bibliography for each chapter at the back of the book.

I probably wouldn't have dived into the science myself if an acquaintance (now friend), who has survived a life-threatening injury himself, had not encouraged me to do so. He also made a bold promise of reward for my suffering that gave me much-needed hope. "You're lucky this happened to you," he said, "because you're going to learn and experience things that you couldn't any other way—amazing, *wonderful* things that most people will go their whole lives without knowing." I'm still not sure about the "lucky" bit, but he was right about the rest of it. I hope I have done justice to the payoff in these pages.

I've retained some names, with permission, and changed all others. I've also changed personally identifying details where appropriate, for instance in describing my fellow hospital patients. I reconstructed events and conversations from memory, aided by medical records and copious journal entries from the accident year, and I sometimes altered minor details to more effectively convey an emotional truth, or to keep action moving at an engaging pace.

BEAUTIFUL TRAUMA

1

·····

An Explosion

in Brooklyn

January 27, 2006. I've stayed awake until 2:30 a.m. obsessively revising a presentation for my new boss, determined to impress him with its elegant clarity in describing the marketing strategy for a new product. When I finally turn on the bathroom faucet to brush my teeth before bed, it issues a screaming jet of air instead of water. With barely a thought, I flush the toilet to check whether all the plumbing is misbehaving.

I hear a loud noise, then notice a tiny spray of blood on the wall—brick red against shiny yellow tiles. Whose is that? Not yet alarmed, I glance right to discover a gaping wound in my forearm, about three and a half inches square, all blood gurgling over black Jell-O and pulled-taffy innards. Instantly, I become disoriented. To the sound of blood slap . . . slap . . . slapping against the floor, I stare at the gash, dumbly assuming that the nature of my predicament will become clear.

The strategy works; I realize that the toilet has exploded,

propelling a sharp hunk of porcelain through the inside of my right wrist, partially severing my dominant hand. This is bad, *really* bad. And it's happening to *me*. I look down to see myself standing in a large puddle of blood, whose rapid expansion begs immediate action. Still, my brain insists on one further second of reflection to mark an irreversible transition: The life I've been living is over. The next one, however long it lasts, begins now.

Decorating the apartment in red as I go, I tear into the bedroom, lurch for the tabletop phone with my left hand, and dial 911 while heading back to the kitchen. I struggle to keep the phone pressed between shoulder and ear as I yank a dirty dish towel off the oven door handle and crumple it into my right wrist. Saturated with blood in seconds, it lands with a *splosh* when I dash it to the floor. I fling open a cabinet, grab a clean towel, and try again, but the blood soaks through that one, too. Realizing I'll never get ahead of it, I wrap another towel around the packed wound, one more around that, then stretch both arms overhead and squeeze the sodden wad as hard as I can with my left hand.

Concurrently describing the nature of the emergency to the 911 operator, I can only convey its magnitude by verbally tracing the trail of blood, which is sprayed in feathery arcs on the walls, dribbling down the floor molding, gumming up the keys of my laptop, soaking into a basket of clean laundry, painting traffic lines on the rug, pooling in my shoes on the floor. And yet, I feel no pain.

The operator reports that an ambulance has been dispatched

and instructs me to stay on the line until it arrives. Certain I'll pass out before then, from loss of blood or simply the horror of the experience, I resolve to enlist a neighbor to meet the paramedics in the lobby of our apartment building, rather than risk the trip myself. I go to the door across the hall and start kicking it, unable to knock.

"Somebody please help—I've had an accident!" After several such pleas, my neighbor opens the door.

"Jesus Christ! Call 911!" he yells over his shoulder into the apartment.

"I've already done that," I murmur. "Someone just needs to let the paramedics in when they get here." I drop the phone at his feet and sink to the hallway floor as other neighbors drift warily out of their apartments.

Kneeling, head bowed and arms held high like a surrendering fugitive, I shiver in my little nightgown, gripping my wrapped wrist so hard both arms shake. I close my eyes, not wanting to see any more. Adrenaline rush gives way to terror, which has a different quality than other emotions I've experienced. These tend to be a mix—of love and protectiveness, anger and shame, gratitude and relief—just as the color black in a painting is rarely pure black, but rather a mixture of black and another dark color like blue or green, added for depth and nuance. This flavor of fear courses through me undiluted and unchecked, obliterating all rational thought. Sweat-slicked and heart banging, I squeeze my eyes tighter and chant softly: "I'm so scared. I'm so scared. I'm so scared . . ."

The neighbors flit around me wordlessly, trying to drape

me with a shawl that won't stay on because they won't get close enough to secure it. Strangely, I don't want them to do anything. I, too, am repelled by my blood-spattered body and—regretting the loss of innocence I imagine they've already suffered for seeing me in such a state—don't want to impose on them any further intimacy with it. I feel beyond rescue, like a stricken, twitching deer on the highway that people drive past, saying, "Nothing we can do, have to let nature take its course." And I feel dangerous, as if my trauma were contagious.

"Don't touch the blood," I feebly warn a neighbor who announces she's entering my apartment to pack a hospital bag for me.

"Becca. It's David from upstairs. What do you need me to do?"

"I've called an ambulance," I reply. "I just need someone to let the paramedics in."

"OK. I'm going downstairs to wait for them. I'll bring them up as soon as they get here."

I drink in David's authoritative voice, acknowledging his words with a nod. He puts his hand on top of my head for a long moment. The warm, confident gesture ever so slightly weakens my swirling fear, a smudge of lapis into black. I feel a little more human, maybe worth saving.

David returns with an army of help from the ambulance service and police and fire departments, the size of the entourage a precaution taken by the 911 operator upon learning my injury resulted from an explosion. The neighbors recede and the paramedics take over, unwrapping, examining, then properly bandaging my wrist, checking my vital signs. Ten minutes later they bundle me onto a stretcher and maneuver it into the elevator. As the doors close I call to a policeman to bring my cell phone and health insurance cards from the workbag beside my bed, and to call my sister, Erica, making him promise to get word to me when he reaches her. As the paramedics lift me into the ambulance, I realize they've never told me I'll be all right. Guessing they aren't sure, I wish they'd lied.

The ambulance ride takes just eleven minutes, and the velocity with which we fly over the Brooklyn Bridge creates the sensation of sledding down a steep hill on my back. The sudden lights of the bridge capture my gaze, their glittering strands visible through the back windows from where I lie on the stretcher. My breathing slows as I muse about my love for the landmark. Jerked back to my distress by a sharp turn onto FDR Drive, I hope to lose consciousness, feeling colder and sicker each minute, worried Erica might be traveling on business, dreading my prognosis yet to come. Finally, I start to cry—tired, coughing sobs. Miles, the enormous paramedic attending me, watches silently. With my left hand I grope for one of his, which he lets me hold tightly.

When the ambulance comes to an abrupt halt, Miles and his partner haul my stretcher out of the vehicle and push it through a large set of swinging doors. Noting the ceiling change from the poured cement of the ambulance bay to the fluorescent lights of the emergency room, I will myself to stop crying. My pride has poked through the veil of shock, and I want the doctors to think me strong and helpful. My best friend, Jen, has counseled me in difficult times: "Act how you want to feel, and you'll eventually feel that way." So I do.

Several emergency room staff catch up with my stretcher and stride purposefully alongside to guide it to an open bay. They all begin to work on me at once, checking blood pressure, unwrapping the wound, taking my medical history, administering a tetanus shot, removing clothing and jewelry that obstruct their efforts. One nurse, almost tenderly, sets about swabbing the blood off my face, chest, hands, and feet. I appreciate the quiet, matter-of-fact way they question me and instruct one another. Leaning my head back on the pillow, I lift my eyes from the tangle of faces and hands surrounding my wrist and gaze softly ahead of me.

A minute later, Erica appears at my feet. Advancing into the bay, she glances at my open wrist, which lies on a table to the right of the bed like a half-carved roast on a platter. She recovers with a wan smile and takes my left hand. Her presence reminds me of our collective strength and resilience, rigorously tested by numerous family crises. She is here. I can handle anything now. Even the prospect of death, if that's what's in store. I smile back at her, and my fear recedes. Then, at last, pain erupts in its place—a burning car parked on my hand, vicious proof of life.

2

·····

Fight or Flight?
Our Built-In
Threat-Defense Program

I regret that, in telling the story of that night over the years, I have destroyed countless people's peaceful relationships with their toilets. I know this because they say so ("Becca, I think of you *every time I go to the bathroom!*"), before fishing for reassurance that such a catastrophe could never befall them. Sadly, I can't provide it, since the cause of the explosion remains unknown. I can only offer my annoyingly incomplete hypothesis, based on some Google bingeing and the best guess of a plumber's son I met at a party, that it involved excess air pressure in the system that flushed the building's toilets from a giant water tank in the basement. So if your toilet is flushed by water from its own little commode-top tank, you can probably exhale now.

What I do know is that my injury posed an existential threat. If I hadn't acted as I did, I might have bled to death, or lost enough blood to suffer permanent damage to my brain and other vital organs. Nobody would have come looking for me in time to prevent any of that. My neighbors, conditioned to ignore mysterious, big-city noises, slept through the brief blast. Colleagues and friends would have assumed they'd missed some explanatory email from me when I failed to show up for that Friday workday or a weekend meal, and my family wouldn't have expected to hear from me for days. For all anyone knows, then, I saved my own life. Or at the least, life as I knew and wanted it to be.

People admire me for this feat. *I* admire me for this feat. I've inwardly gloated about it in infuriating or demoralizing situations, like when I had to sit with my "feedback is a gift" face on for fifteen minutes while a boss explained that I am not a creative thinker (I disagree). Ah, so that's what you think of me? No matter. *I've* saved my own life. But while the admiration feels good, it also discomfits, and not only because so many people dislike women who own their achievements. More so because it implicitly credits me with consciously orchestrating every step of my escape from danger, ignoring the extensive role of factors beyond my control—beginning with the brain's built-in threat-defense program.

Nerve cells, or neurons, play a starring role in the threat-defense program. Neurons' raison d'être is to relay data, in the form of electrochemical transmissions, throughout the brain and body. While they take slightly different forms depending on their location and purpose, you can imagine their fundamental anatomy as that of a dandelion gone to seed: there's a cell body (dandelion head) covered in dendrites (the fluff on the head) and a skinny, stemlike projection from the cell body called an *axon*, which has branches at its end, like roots. (This is an imperfect analogy, as dendrites are actually thicker than axons, but it's good enough for our purposes.) The structures we call *nerves* are actually bundles of axons.

When adjacent neurons communicate, one neuron generates an electrical impulse that travels from the top of its axon through to its branching ends. There, the impulse stimulates the release of chemicals, which diffuse across a tiny, fluid-filled gap to react with the dendrites of neighboring neurons. Reactions above a certain threshold cause those neighboring neurons to generate their own electrical impulses, leading to stimulation of other neurons in their vicinity, and so on. Such communication transpires on an unfathomably large scale. Estimates peg the number of neurons in the human nervous system at around 100 billion, and a single neuron typically communicates with ten thousand others. The result is trillions of neuron-to-neuron connections. If we could hear it, the chatter among them would be deafening.

Neurons are the workhorses of the central nervous system (which comprises the brain and spinal cord) and of the peripheral nervous system (the network of nerves that permeates the skin, muscles, and organs). Communicating via neurons, the central and peripheral nervous systems form a feedback loop that enables collection and processing of data about the body's internal and external environment, and coordination of the body's responses to it, whether automatic or consciously deliberated.

Within the brain, different groups of neurons—neural neighborhoods, if you will—specialize in processing particular types of data, for instance that related to visual stimuli. And specific neural neighborhoods routinely collaborate to carry out specific processing tasks, like the threat-defense program.

How did all this work to my advantage? At the instant of the explosion, several neural neighborhoods involved in the threat-defense program leapt to work, crunching data about the sights, sounds, and bodily impact of the event to synthesize a detailed account of it. One of them—the amygdala—also compared rudimentary facts about the event to situations tagged "dangerous" in my evolutionary programming and memory. Discovering troubling similarities, it triggered a full-body response to help me cope with the danger I faced.

Muscles all over my body contracted, freezing me in readiness to assume whatever posture the situation demanded next. Natural opioids flowed into my spinal cord, blocking pain-triggering sensory nerve signals en route to the brain for processing. My breathing quickened and adrenaline flowed into my bloodstream, boosting supplies of blood glucose—muscles' main source of energy. My heart pumped faster to speed distribution of the surplus energy throughout my body, and blood vessels channeled it into my limbs (where it would likely be needed most) by constricting themselves in my abdomen and skin, and relaxing in my arms and legs.

Body thus poised and fueled, a cascade of chemical reactions in my brain whipped up its processing rigor, and the whole organ kicked into a state of high alert, consumed by the work of monitoring the situation and sustaining my physical preparedness. Fear—thought to occur when the bodily symptoms of this state bubble into consciousness—failed to transpire.

Within milliseconds of the blast, the threat-defense program had transformed me from a groggy corporate climber into a hypervigilant animal, hell-bent on survival and primed for action. But *what* action? The threat-defense program can automatically initiate a handful of survival strategies that have proven helpful throughout human history, famously including freezing, fleeing, and fighting (negotiations with blood-thirsty predators, I gather, routinely fall apart). It can also initiate strategies that an individual has learned, like the battle-field injury-management protocols that soldiers internalize through extensive drilling. Such stock strategies are fast, and effective to a point . . . then one needs to address the particulars of a situation.

That's when the cerebral cortex—the wormy outer layer of the brain, which specializes in tough processing jobs—jumps in to bang out a bespoke survival strategy. I experienced the process as a lightning round of straightforward decision-making: Wait for help, or take action? Stop the bleeding first, or call 911 first? Bind the wound with a terry-cloth bathroom towel or a linen dish towel? End to end, however, contemporary science suggests it was much more complex.

At every decision point, my cortex drew on processing capacity and information throughout the brain to define a range of possible actions. Then it assessed and ranked each according to potential survival benefit, identified the best bet, and commanded my body to carry it out. Concurrently, processing loops strengthened by the threat-defense program provided my cortex with granular feedback about the impact of each action taken, for incorporation into the developing strategy.

Neuroscientists don't fully understand how the cortex manages all this. But many agree that several mutually influential human assets play a critical role. One of these is language, which, as asserted by contemporary philosopher Daniel Dennett, "lays down tracks on which thoughts can travel." For instance, with the pronouns *I* and *me*, language gives us the concept of a *self*—an entity that acts and is acted upon—and with verb tenses, it gives us the concepts of past, present, and future, thus the possibility of a self that persists over time. Other assets crucial to planning include the type of consciousness that makes us aware of, and able to reflect upon, our selves and our experience (versus simply being awake), and our capacity for storing and recalling facts and personal history in memory.

Interacting in innumerable ways, language, consciousness, and memory allow us to recognize both physical and conceptual phenomena that concern us. They enable us to construct multistep plans for addressing the problems and opportunities we face, and to apply knowledge we've acquired about our selves and the world in doing so. And they endow us with the superpower of mental time travel, so that we can project our selves into the future to explore the potential consequences of those plans.

I had the sense of deliberately leveraging these assets during my escape. Wait for help, or act to save myself? Knowing I lived alone, and that blood loss can lead to death, I imagined waiting for help. I saw myself slumped dead against the inside of my apartment door—a blurry mash-up of dark-green paint, pale limbs, and a blood-soaked purple silk chemise—and knew I had to act. Stop the bleeding first, or call 911 first? Knowing I'd never dealt with a gushing wound before, I saw myself trying, failing, and heaped against the door again, no help on the way. I called 911 first. And so on, with each di-lemma that sprang to mind, until I finally delivered myself into the care of my horrified neighbors.

I wish I could explain that sense of deliberate decision-making in terms of the cortex's operations (cue empathetic belly laugh from neuroscientists and philosophers everywhere). But the precise means by which conscious experience arises and influences nonconscious brain activity is the subject of many vigorously debated theories, rather than scientific fact. So, I can't explain. And that's fine, because in studying and pondering the subject, I've concluded that whatever my conscious contribution to my survival that night, that's not what's admirable in the story.

What's admirable is the capacity nature has endowed humanity with to confront novel, life-threatening events with time-tested survival strategies, and the creativity to improvise new ones on the spot. We needn't be privileged to possess it, or extraordinary to leverage it. Ubiquitous and renewable, it's available from an early age, and automatically activated as often as necessary. It doesn't guarantee survival, of course; we are mortal, after all. But like gods bursting onto the scene of a Greek drama, it can deliver us from the most seemingly hopeless scenarios. And in this one, it gave me a second life.

3

Diagnosis:

Spaghetti Wrist

"Can I have something for the pain?" I say, to no one in particular in the throng around me.

"No one's given you anything yet?" a nurse responds, surprised.

"No."

The nurse asks how I'd rate my pain on a scale from one to ten, one being mild discomfort and ten being "the worst pain you could ever imagine feeling in your life." I can imagine pretty unbearable pain—say, that induced by surgery before the invention of anesthesia, or by being boiled alive like that miserable sod in the novel *Shōgun*. My pain is intense but bearable, so I rate it a four.

The nurse disappears momentarily and returns with a big syringe of morphine.

"This is going to pinch a little," she warns, clearly from habit, as she can't possibly believe a shot could be worse than a hole in the arm, "then you'll feel a cold sensation in your chest."

Sure enough, a frigid wave rushes from my left shoulder, through my chest, and down my right arm. It's bizarre, and amazing, to feel something *inside* that part of the body, like when a hot drink burns down the esophagus, calling attention to the organ's existence. Suddenly, I don't care about the pain. It hasn't gone away; I just don't care about it. Rather, I feel the same quietly joyful "there's no place I'd rather be" contentment I have felt lingering in the arms of someone I love. I believe I finally understand the reason people abuse narcotics. It must be because the feeling is *just that good*, worth risking a whole lot to experience. I'm none too happy a mere hour later, however, when the morphine wears off. The pain has proved itself a screaming seven at least, which the nurse doesn't seem surprised to hear when Erica tells her.

Enjoying a second, healthier dose of morphine, I note that the crowd of staff around me has dissipated, leaving two young men in scrubs.

"I'm Dr. Goldstein, and this is Dr. Schwartz," the taller, dark-haired, blue-eyed one announces. "Ha. Sounds like a Lower East Side comedy team," he adds under his breath, chuckling. "*Anyway*. So, what happened here?"

I tell the story, which Erica hears for the first time along with the doctors, and can't help laughing as I do. It's impossible to talk about an exploding toilet with a straight face.

"*Seriously?!* That's incredible!" Dr. Goldstein says. He's

clearly the more senior physician, as he leads the conversation while Dr. Schwartz sits to the side, listening. "I've *never* heard anything that crazy, and believe me, we see it all here. Well, I knew something big was gonna happen tonight because I couldn't sleep in the on-call room, and now here you are. So let's get you taken care of."

Dr. Goldstein's jovial manner makes me think there might be cause for optimism about my prognosis, so I muster the courage to ask about it. "Am I . . . going to lose my hand?" I look back and forth between him and Erica, who encourages me with her eyes. She wants to know, too.

"Definitely not," he says.

"Oh, thank *God*. Will I need a blood transfusion?"

"Nope."

"Really? But there was so much blood . . ."

"Body has five liters of blood in it, and you gotta lose more than one before you need a transfusion. Believe it or not, you didn't lose enough. Must've looked like it, though. Arteries really spray." They sure do.

Erica and I look at each other with relief. The worst-case scenarios thus off the table, we interest ourselves in the long process by which Dr. Goldstein, with Dr. Schwartz assisting, assesses the extent of damage to my wrist. Only, I stare straight ahead to avoid glimpsing the gore, having seen enough already.

First, Dr. Goldstein cleans the wound by placing my right forearm in a square plastic receptacle he's rested on my stomach and dumping a gallon of some liquid over it. "Oh, ewwww!" I moan, seeing a rusty red wave surge against the sides of the container with my peripheral vision. When will the nastiness stop? Erica and Dr. Goldstein laugh. "That's not blood, it's iodine!" they assure me, nearly in concert.

Next, a technician using a mobile unit brought to my bedside x-rays my hand and wrist in several awkward positions, checking for broken bones. Then Dr. Goldstein performs a Doppler ultrasound of my hand's arteries to determine whether the artery thought to be severed receives any blood flow. The amplified sound of my blood pulsing through the vessels—WHEE-ew, WHEE-ew, WHEE-ew, WHEE-ew—resembles that of a fetal heartbeat, at least as I've heard it on TV. The poignant irony that I am hearing this sound for the first time at the age of thirty-nine as a result of an accident, not a pregnancy, does not escape me.

Erica stays with me during these disgusting procedures—fighting nausea, she later admits—despite several invitations by Dr. Goldstein to step outside the curtained bay until the worst is done. Finally, he sits in a chair next to me and asks me to make a few simple gestures with my hand, as he'll get some indication of which tendons in my wrist are severed by whether I can execute his instructions.

"So," he says afterward, leaning back in the chair. "Would you like me to tell you what we've learned so far?"

"Please," I reply.

He speaks just a few sentences, then pauses. I hear the words *tendons, artery, severed,* but can't glean the larger implications of what he's said, though he has taken care to speak in layman's terms. I ask him to repeat what he's said, then turn it over in my head again. Still, I understand little. The foreign context provides few clues, and the morphine can't be helping me follow them.

"Would you like to hear more right now," Dr. Goldstein asks, "or do you want some time to absorb what I've said so far?"

I hesitate in responding. What *do* I want? "Yeah—I could use a little time to think about that, thanks." I can't remember even one instance when I haven't wanted more information on a topic that concerned or interested me, but clearly I will need to learn a lot more about my injury before I understand even a little about its impact.

"OK, we'll pick it up a little later, then," he says, smiling. He stands and turns to Dr. Schwartz. "Let's have the chief come take a look at this."

"He's got clinic starting at one this afternoon. I'll book her in on the early side," Dr. Schwartz offers.

"I want him to see her sooner than that," Dr. Goldstein counters. "We can pull him off rounds at seven this morning." Dr. Schwartz confirms the plan, and the two disappear behind the bay's curtains to attend to some other unlucky arrival.

For the next several hours, a continuous stream of people parades past my bedside—Miles the paramedic coming to wish me well on his way out, nurses checking on my morphine, and surgical residents (four or five of them, I lose track) checking out my "spaghetti wrist," as Dr. Goldstein has told me my injury is called, due to the numerous severed, strand-like structures involved.

The string of surgical "consults" makes a great parody of speed dating. Each resident initiates the same conversation: "Can you do this, this, this? Feel this, this, this?" he asks. "Yes, no, no. Sort of, no, no," I reply. Within seven minutes he's decided whether my case is sexy enough to warrant follow-up, while I've admired the beginnings of a talented clinician, or written the guy off for lousy bedside manner and cowardice in the face of icky wounds. Then we never see each other again.

As time drags on, I begin to think that each new resident stopping by must be the chief, and I am disappointed each time I'm proven wrong. Then I see him—it *has* to be him—crossing the emergency room toward my bed. His compact runner's body cuts cleanly through the zigzagging people and rolling beds in his path with no extraneous motion, no drag, and a momentary hush falls over the room while everyone seemingly tracks his progress.

Still loath to look at my wound, I watch from the corner of my eye as he settles himself on the edge of the chair next to my bed. Confirming my guess that he is indeed Dr. Vargas, chief resident of the hospital's esteemed hand-surgery team, a handful of junior residents quickly clusters around him, presumably waiting for him to speak. He does not. Instead, he remains silent for a long time while, I imagine, he reviews my chart and contemplates my wrist. Stealing a glance at him, I am confronted by an expressionless face, bookish glasses, and a penetrating stare. I turn away.

Without sharing his conclusions, he turns his attention to the question of tendon function, repeating the tests Dr. Goldstein performed to form a preliminary diagnosis.

"Make a fist?" His voice is quiet but assured, a bit nasal with a hint of New York.

I flex all the right muscles but don't know if I've succeeded because my hand is numb and I'm still not looking at it.

"Touch your thumb to your little finger?" I wonder what happens when I try. Eventually the positions he wants to see become too difficult to describe. He needs to show them to me from where he sits, so he can keep his eyes trained on my hand and register its slightest movements.

He asks softly, "Do you think you can look?"

I steel myself, then spend the next ten minutes attempting to copy his gestures, watching the pearly ends of the cut tendons in my forearm reach in vain for their lost mates on the other side of the deep, burgundy wound. The sight is disturbing, yet perversely intriguing.

His exam completed, Dr. Vargas explains that an artery, major nerve, and numerous tendons enabling finger contraction have been severed in my wrist. They must be surgically "repaired" to the extent possible. He also coolly informs me that because the tendons have been severed near the point in the forearm where they become muscle, some of the ends (or stumps) nearest the muscle may not be strong enough to hold sutures. If not, multiple stumps from the hand will need to be stitched to fewer stumps in the arm, depriving me of independent finger motion in my dominant hand.

"Meaning . . . I'd have a paw," I guess.

"Basically . . . yes," he replies. He offers no reassurance or sympathy, nor any clue as to how he feels about what he's telling me, which makes it hard to know how I should feel about it. Only a wedding ring and a dark, artfully shaped goatee betray any desire on his part to be known.

Dr. Vargas rises, confers quietly with Dr. Goldstein for a moment, then leaves. Erica and I look at each other but say nothing. Concentrating hard on the information Dr. Vargas has conveyed, I conclude that it *should* upset me, but it does not. Significant loss of hand function seems inconsequential, given that just a few hours ago I feared bleeding to death on my bathroom floor. And morphine inures me to anxiety the way a big, fluffy down comforter locks out winter cold. Under its influence, I just can't get too upset about anything.

Dr. Schwartz returns to the bay, and Dr. Goldstein explains to us all that I have been scheduled for surgery at 3:00 p.m.—nearly eight hours later.

"She's stable, but we can't admit her yet," Dr. Schwartz says to Dr. Goldstein. "So I guess we send her home to wait."

Erica and I shoot "What the fuck!" glances at each other.

"She's been through a lot already—I think that's a little too much to ask," Dr. Goldstein says. "We're not too busy; we can keep her off to the side till then."

Erica and I heave sighs of relief.

Dr. Goldstein sits down and leans over my hand to close my wound for the long wait, halving it with the first suture, then halving each resulting gap again and again until my insides disappear, twenty-six stitches in all. I watch, no longer disturbed by the sight.

"So, what made you choose orthopedics?" I ask as he works.

"C'mon!" he exclaims, gesturing to my wound with shrugged shoulders. "That's *so cool!*"

I laugh, perfectly happy to be the subject of a surgeon's fascination. Surely it'll help him do his best. "Yeah, I guess it is," I reply, considering the matter in a new light.

Finished suturing, Dr. Goldstein applies another sterile dressing, then instructs me to keep my arm constantly elevated—until the surgery, and for weeks after—to facilitate drainage of fluids out of my grotesquely swollen hand. Finally, he arranges for some porters to wheel my bed to the quietest part of the emergency room—a dimly lit corner lined with locked supply cabinets.

4
.....

Instrument of Instruments:
Anatomy of the Hand

Millions of years of biological trial and error produced the modern human hand, with each generation of our ancestors along the way including some individuals born with hands that differed from the norm for the species. The differences, or variations, made these individuals better or worse equipped to cope with their environment's challenges, like predators and hostile terrain, or to take advantage of its opportunities, like new food sources requiring novel mining techniques.

As the phenomenon of natural selection would have it, individuals lucky enough to be born with advantageous hand variations were more likely to survive until they could reproduce and transmit the happy traits to their offspring. Individuals born without such variations—or worse, with variations that made it harder for them to hunt, gather, and escape the neighborhood bad guys—were less likely to survive and reproduce, so their suboptimal hand anatomy died with them.

Over time the advantageous variations became the norm, and the hand we know and love today—praised by Aristotle as the "instrument of instruments"—is evolution's best bet (to date) at what we need in a hand to survive until we can do our part to propagate the species.

So what are the winning anatomical characteristics? Starting from the inside out, our hands boast a remarkably flexible frame constructed of twenty-seven bones (more than any other part of the body, edging the foot out by just one) arranged into five slender digits. Its flexibility comes from the number and variety of joints connecting these bones, which allow the digits and wrist to hinge and rotate in such a way that we can open our hands wide, and reach for and curl our hands around objects of many different sizes and shapes.

Interwoven with the bones, a large number of collaborating structures share an incredibly small space. These include over thirty muscles, attached to the bones of the hand by their thin, sinewy ends, called *tendons*; a complex network of blood vessels, permeating every tissue of the hand and providing the energy required for movement; and peripheral nerves, which, as you may recall from chapter 2, form a feedback loop with the central nervous system.

All this is neatly kitted out in a layer of skin, whose properties and benefits vary depending on where it lies on the frame of the hand and go well beyond physicians' old adage that it merely "keeps blood in, rain out." For starters, skin on the palm of the hand is some of the thickest on the body—second only to that on the sole of the foot—which helps protect it against mechanical stress. It's also "quilted" to facilitate gripping—that is, lined with fat to increase our comfort when holding angular objects, and tethered tightly to the bone at regular intervals (finger joints, lines across the palm) to contain the fat in cushions so that objects can't "ride" the fat across the whole of the palm.

If you have little considered this helpful characteristic, try this brief experiment (Go ahead! I do it all the time as I write, like a cookbook writer testing their recipes. People stare but never say anything . . . or almost never): Place your fingertips firmly on the skin anywhere on your palm, then try to push the skin back and forth. Notice how little it moves? Now try the same thing with the skin of your forearm. See how far your fingers ride back and forth on the more mobile skin? You couldn't reliably hold or maneuver objects if they could travel that much in the grip of your hands.

Then there's the texture of the skin. Papillary ridges, the thickened bands of skin that form our whorling fingerprints, actually cover the entire palm of the hand, as well as the soles of the feet. They aid grasping by acting as tread on a tire, displacing liquids on wet objects so the skin can connect directly with them, instead of hydroplaning around. They also house ducts that secrete sweat, a little of which lubricates the skin and helps it adhere to a surface (like when you lick your fingertips to turn the page of a book); a lot of which might make you drop things. I rued this cruel fact as a young violinist when my hands sweated before recitals, plaguing me with fears of a fumbled bow or botched arpeggios, until I began playing and the music absorbed me.

Perhaps the most thoughtful innovation in the hand's gripping tool kit is the skin's ability to form calluses where repetitive chafing against objects might otherwise cause pain or dysfunction. I appreciated this characteristic, too, as a rower in college. Only, back then, the calluses never seemed to form quickly enough at the beginning of the season, so we winced through initial practices, pulling with raw palms on splintery wooden oars as our skin took its sweet time thickening up.

Flipping to the back of the hand, looser skin than that of the palm can stretch over a clenching fist or retract in folds around the knuckles. Fingernails protect and reinforce our pulpy, vulnerable fingertips and come in handy for scratching itches, peeling Scotch tape off gifts, and other mundane, picky endeavors.

Together, these structural characteristics not only give hands their nearly infinite utility, they also count among the most distinguishing aspects of our unique identities, to which we as individuals, and those around us, relate and even gravitate.

My mother's hands used to intrigue me, back when I was a child standing just about eye level with the kitchen counter, seeing even more of them in a day than I probably did of her face. I watched them intently, noticing the carefully shaped, medium-length oval nails she tended with a worn, burgundy leather manicure kit she'd received as a gift in college from

her mother. As she worked her way around the kitchen preparing meals, I followed the sparkling trajectory of her modest
diamond engagement ring, and visually traced the mint-green
latticework of her prominent veins. When I got the chance—at
church, for instance, where, in the inconvenient absence of
toys, Mom indulged most any activity that kept us kids quiet—
I liked to stroke her veins' velvety twists and turns, and com-
press them to see where the blood went when its path was
obstructed.

Beyond their visual appeal, though, what entranced me
most about Mom's hands was the speed, assurance, and flair
with which they moved. I was filled with awe and questions
watching them perform the most mundane tasks, like dialing
a rotary phone (*How does her finger always know* exactly *where
to go?*), shaking a thermometer to bring the mercury down
(*How come it doesn't fly out of her hands?!*), paring a peeled
orange from top to bottom into perfect, juicy, fan-shaped sec-
tions (*Why doesn't she cut herself?!*). Then there was her quirky
practice of hesitating with a pen over the spot of paper where
she intended to write, and scratching out a couple of tiny "air
letters" with its tip before committing her thoughts to ink, and
the repertoire of animated gestures she used (and still does)
to dramatize her conversations with grown-ups and children
alike.

Best of all was how she used those perfectly shaped fingernails to lull me to sleep when childish, and sometimes not so
childish, worries made me restless. Lightly tracing patterns on

my back and combing through my hair with them, she'd tell me stories that always began "When I was a little girl . . ." and assure me that "things will look better in the morning" as I drifted into a sound sleep from which I generally awoke feeling better indeed. So there's a truth that even a five-year-old knows: More than their impressive construction, it's what hands *do* that makes them essential.

Hand function has four core components: movement, including both the shape hands can make and their range of motion, plus sensation, strength, and dexterity. Hand movements are typically classified as either prehensile or nonprehensile. Primates, including us humans, differ from most other mammals in that we bring our food to our mouths to eat, instead of bringing our mouths to our food. Some other mammals, like raccoons, squirrels, and the mean little gerbils my family kept when I was a kid, bring food to their mouths, too. But whereas they must grasp it between their two paws, like a basketball player about to make a pass, we can wrap the fingers and thumb of just one hand around a hunk of edibles, grasp it to our palm, and bring it to our mouths. This is an example of prehensile movement, and we owe it to our famously opposable thumbs, which can both hinge and rotate, and therefore swing out and across the palm to meet curling fingertips "head-on."

While we employ prehensility to hold objects of an infinite variety of shapes, the grips involved mainly boil down to two: the power grip and the precision grip. While not entirely distinct, they differ in important ways. A power grip encloses its object between the palm and full length of the fingers, with thumb in opposition to buttress them or "lock" the object in place, facilitating application of force to the task at hand, whereas a precision grip encloses its object between the tips of opposing thumb and fingers, without contacting the palm, facilitating delicate manipulation.

Examples of both abound here in my local pub in London, where I write today: the barman pulling a pint of lukewarm London Pride ale (power grip); a woman tucking into a traditional Sunday roast, using her knife to push slabs of beef and Yorkshire pudding onto the back of her fork (precision grip); a server loosening the stubborn lid on a screw-top jar of cocktail olives (power grip), then spinning it off (precision grip).

Exhibiting nonprehensile movement, whereby the hand acts on an object without holding it, we have the barman now punching keys on the cash register to ring up that ale, a server pushing tables together to accommodate a large party coming to watch "the football" (which will always be "soccer" to me) on TV, and a dad dabbing a bit of dinner off his toddler's face with a napkin-wrapped index finger while his partner scrolls through content on an iPad.

Before movement, the nervous system crackles with activity. As discussed in chapter 2, nerves are actually bundles of axons, the stemlike part of a neuron. The axons in peripheral nerves stretch all the way from their cell bodies in, or near, the spinal cord to the specific patch of skin, muscle, or organ the neuron serves. Some peripheral neurons convey movement commands from the central nervous system to muscles throughout the body (motor neurons), and others convey data to the central nervous system about the body's internal and external environment (sensory neurons).

The sensory nervous system is meticulously structured to do justice to our infinitely sensual world. Different types of sensory data—about the form, texture, and temperature of external stimuli and their mechanical impact on our bodies, about how our skin stretches and hearts pumps, and more— are captured by axon endings tailored to their unique tasks. For instance, axon endings called Merkel disks register the curves, edges, and textures of objects we come into contact with, and axon endings called Meissner corpuscles register the microslips of objects across our skin. When we hold an object, this data helps the central nervous system automatically adjust our hand position and grip strength so that we don't drop or crush it. Also, most sensory neurons convey just one type of data to the central nervous system, with their transmission speed and frequency optimized to do so.

The central nervous system then blends the peripheral nervous system data streams and other sensory input, such as visual and audio data, and translates it into an account—of which we may or may not be conscious—of what's going on with our bodies, so that we can respond appropriately. The sensory experiences we recognize as pain, vibration, temperature, and texture count among our conscious perceptions, as do a few others to which most of us have given little, if any, thought. One of these is proprioception, the ability to sense the position of our body in space—in other words, knowing versus seeing that our arm is outstretched to hail a taxi (in New York) or a bus (in London)—which the brain cleverly deduces from the tension in our skin, muscles, and other internal structures.

Another is localization of stimuli, the ability to pinpoint the precise position on the body where we have come into contact with external stimuli. When I know without looking that I've just stabbed the pad of my left thumb with the lead of a mechanical pencil while blindly rummaging through my purse in search of house keys, it's localization delivering the bad news. Precisely how the neural activity resulting from such tactile stimulation leads to our conscious experience of it is, so far, as mysterious to neuroscientists as the emergence of any other conscious state, including our emotions.

Hands are sensory SUVs, guzzling up massive amounts of tactile data—data so voluminous and crucial to human survival and thriving that it claims a huge share of the brain's sensory processing capacity, relative to that claimed by other body parts, even the much larger arms and legs. Receptor-dense fingertips and a profusion of axon endings throughout the skin of the palm are key enablers of the guzzling. And remember papillary ridges? They contribute, too, increasing the hand's surface area, and thus receptors' exposure to external stimuli—even more so when we sweat, causing the papillary ridges to swell.

These unique aspects of the hand help explain why we can discriminate so finely between, and take pleasure in, so many tactile sensations at our fingertips. Consider the differences in feel between furry dog tummy and silky toddler hair, bubble wrap and corrugated cardboard, a handful of raw carrot sticks and a handful of raw hamburger meat. We struggle to comprehend sensations (or sounds or colors, for that matter) described in words. Yet we comprehend them instantly with our hands, and particularly the fingertips, and with a richness and subtlety only they can convey. If you need proof, try another experiment: Draw your fingertips across your cheek a few times and think about what they're telling you. Is your skin smooth or bumpy? Moist or dry? Taut or lax? Now draw the inside of your wrist across your cheek. Much less tactile information, right?

Rounding out the core components of hand function, strength enables us to apply force against resistance; and dexterity—the product of movement, sensation, strength, and the brain's capacity to plan—is the hand's ability to effect small, precise movements, like those required to fasten a button or write with a pen.

Put all this complex, purpose-built structure and functionality together and we have an extraordinary machine in (and on) our hands. How does the brain drive it? To illustrate, let's say I want to drop a physical issue of my guilty pleasure, *Hello!* magazine, onto the recycling pile. My brain issues a "trash that twaddle" command to my spinal cord in a way that determines the most efficient activation of the peripheral motor nerves serving the muscles involved. The spinal cord relays the command to the nerves, the nerves activate the muscles, and the muscles obediently contract, tugging on their terminal tendons. The tendons tug on the bones in the hand to which they are affixed, and the bone frame assumes the position required to drop the magazine.

Ahead of the mechanics, however, the brain must "decide" to move the body. And as exemplified by the threat-defense program explored in chapter 2, even the most apparently simple maneuver—drop a magazine, call 911, grab a dish towel—is the product of an astonishing amount of brain processing, processing informed not only by our sensing of the "here and now," but also to various degrees by our evolutionary programming, life experience, knowledge, imagination, goals, physical ability, and any other ready inputs the brain deems relevant.

Apparently, then, the only "say" the hand has in its own deployment is the contribution of sensory data. So is it just a puppet on strings pulled by the brain, dutifully playing the bit part our know-it-all gray matter writes for it in our pursuit of health and happiness?

Far from it. Indeed, anthropologists and neuroscientists widely believe that the hand helped create the modern brain. As the hand evolved and allowed our ancestors to gain greater control over their environment (using found objects as tools for hunting and gathering, for instance), their brains needed to develop the intellectual horsepower necessary to navigate through the more complex and demanding situations the evolving hand presented. Simultaneously, the brain's increasing capability led to more sophisticated and successful strategies for survival, from toolmaking to building and living within a collaborative society.

So interdependent are hand and brain, in fact, that we cannot explore the realm, method, and influence of one without exploring those of the other. And delving into all of that, we soon encounter tricky, even uncomfortable, questions about ourselves—like why we perceive, feel, believe, and do what we do. Consider these questions in the context of a traumatic injury, and what began as a seemingly straightforward study of the hand becomes a life-changing endeavor.

5

My Family Flies
to My Side

For the better part of the day, I drift in and out of consciousness while Erica tackles some of the many important administrative tasks necessitated by the accident, intently tapping
emails out on her BlackBerry and occasionally leaving for the
ambulance bay, where cell phone calls are allowed. She keeps
me briefed on her progress with a constant, cheerful patter.

"Mom and Dad should both be here by the time you get
out of surgery," she reports. We have delayed notifying our
parents until now, partly hopeful that the news will be less
worrisome if delivered with a diagnosis and treatment plan,
perhaps also reluctant to set in motion events that will bring
them together for only the second time since their acrimoni-
ous divorce five years ago.

"How did Mom take the news?" I ask. Fiercely loving, Mom
had been deeply concerned by lesser threats to her children's
health and happiness when we were growing up.

"Fine, so I knew it hadn't sunk in," Erica replies, scanning incoming emails. Then she looks up, frowning. "But when she called back with her flight plans, she told me she almost threw up when it hit her how seriously hurt you were."

While Mom's response to this particular trauma seems perfectly appropriate, her distress in any situation pains Erica and me greatly, and our lifelong desire to preclude it must have contributed to the development of our ability to remain calm and competent in a crisis.

Erica smiles at the BlackBerry. "My friend Adam Googled Dr. Vargas for us." I suspect she has a crush on Adam, and hope his support means the feeling is mutual. Maybe once her own divorce is further behind her, she can marry him.

"OK, here's what he found out." She reads aloud: "Licensed in New York State . . . good, no board certifications . . . don't know what that means . . . graduated from med school in 2001. So that makes him . . . early thirtysomething. Wow."

"Huh, quite the spring chicken," I say. "Seems like he knows what he's doing, though . . . right?"

"Yeah," Erica says, looking up, "and when I talked to your internist this morning, he said Bellevue specializes in injuries like yours, and that it sounds like you're getting excellent care."

"Well, that's good, since I don't have a whole lotta choice at this point," I respond, momentarily sobered to think of how much of my future rests, literally, in the hands of strangers. "I'm going to start a foundation," I proclaim, to chase off darker thoughts, "to help victims of toilet accidents around the world overcome their embarrassment. I'll call it . . . the Toilet Emergency Association. TEA!"

Erica laughs. "And to raise money, you can sell white rubber bracelets with little dangling toilet charms on them." We are both laughing loudly now, and I wonder what "the neighbors"— a couple of guarded prisoners cuffed to gurneys nearby—think of our unlikely exuberance. Bellevue is the designated hospital for people incarcerated at New York's Rikers Island jail complex, as well as officers of "New York's Finest" police force. Presumably the two parties don't share rooms.

Removing an elastic band from her wrist, Erica stands up and steps forward. "Here," she says, gathering my long, heavy hair into a ponytail on top of my head. "You're getting tangled in it. Better?"

"Much," I reply gratefully as she returns to her seat. "I just wish I didn't look so bad." Physically incapacitated and stripped to my underwear beneath the sheets, I feel uncharacteristically self-conscious.

"Is it the morphine talking, or is there an inordinate number of ridiculously good-looking doctors around here?"

"*Yes!*" Erica yelps in agreement, rocking forward and slapping her knee. "It's unreal—like a Hollywood rom-com or something."

Sensing my genuine discomfort, she rummages in her purse for some makeup and stands up again. Dotting concealer under my dark-rimmed eyes and smudging a bit of gloss on my lips, she adds, "But hey, your pedicure looks hot."

At 3:00 p.m., a doctor we've not yet met rolls me and my bed, followed by Erica, through a labyrinth of corridors and up in an elevator to a curtained bay outside an operating room. There, Erica and I construct a long list of questions to ask Dr. Vargas about the imminent surgery while I clumsily sign legal authorizations for the procedure with my nondominant left hand. Suddenly, he and his three assisting residents appear in a crowd of slate-blue scrubs at the foot of my bed. Their matching shower caps look both comical and foreboding.

"Do you have any questions before we go in?" Dr. Vargas asks, eyes darting upward to the clock on the wall behind us.

"Yes," I reply emphatically.

He folds his arms across his chest and listens intently as I launch into a series of inquiries about the procedure, the decisions he would need to make in its course, the best and worst possible outcomes. His responses are measured, detailed, and in terms I can grasp despite the foreign subject matter. When he does not know the answer to a question, he says so.

Finally, I ask the question that weighs heaviest on my mind: "And, uh, how many times have you guys done this?"

"I lead a team of surgeons that performs about eighty tendon or nerve repairs a month."

"That's great! Now, please don't take this the wrong way, but . . . how many have *you personally* done?"

Dr. Vargas pauses just a beat. I think I notice him draw a small breath and wonder if he is calculating the many qualifying events or, realizing his response will inspire either fear or confidence, picking an impressive number to cite. "About a hundred."

My internist has advised that any number above twenty is favorable, so I'm satisfied by this response. Then it occurs to me that I didn't ask how many spaghetti wrists he's operated on, but I push the thought aside. Time is of the essence. "Awesome. Let's do it," I exclaim, as if I have a choice. The team promptly wheels me into the operating room, where I dutifully count back from ten and succumb to general anesthesia.

I awake that evening in a silent, white recovery room, shrouded by a gray curtain drawn partially around my bed. The large, empty space amplifies my sense of estrangement, and my chest feels as though someone has been jumping on it. I find my right arm propped over my head, hand and forearm dressed in lightly plastered gauze that covers the surgeons' tracks, hinting at nothing of their success or failure. Thankfully, Erica soon arrives.

"Hey . . . how're you feeling?" she asks, pulling back the curtain and hugging me gently.

"Crappy," I croak. "How'd it go?"

"Dr. Vargas says there was more damage than they thought, so it took longer than expected—about three and a half hours. But they were able to do everything they needed to." I want to know more but am too exhausted to ask questions, too mentally hazy to digest more information.

Presently, two dark shapes obscuring the distant doorway

come into focus, revealing my approaching parents. I can tell from their screwed-up faces that I look as awful as I feel.

"Oh, love," Mom says, teary-eyed as she leans down to kiss my cheek.

"Wow, kid, that's an impressive cast," Dad says, reaching in to smooth my hair. His eyes shine, too. I receive my parents' greetings with a smile, relishing their unexpectedly reassuring presence, and forgetting to worry about how they will tolerate each other, or how Mom will stomach the story of the accident, which Erica begins to tell as I hover on the edge of sleep.

I next awake an hour later, in a room in the surgical recovery ward where I will spend the night. Dad has gone to meet my stepmother, Kate, at their hotel, and Erica prepares to head home for some sleep after her fifteen-hour shift of vigilance on my behalf. Both will return in the morning, and Mom will stay in the empty bed next to mine, though I haven't asked her to. Chronically independent, I don't like to ask for help, nor does it often occur to me that any might be available. But I don't want to be alone just now, so I'll let Mom mother me, at least for the night.

We don't sleep much. Rather, I muse aloud in a semi-coherent, stream-of-consciousness monologue about my hopes for a strong recovery, trying to convince myself that I can live a good life even without one. Mom, always indulgent of my philosophical jaunts, follows along, occasionally interjecting practical encouragement I desperately need to hear: "You're a hard worker, love. You'll do the best you can, then you'll adjust to whatever happens." Twice she fetches nurses to shoot me up with more morphine when its efficacy begins to wane. When we see the sun rising—a neon, pink-orange flood through Queens—I note with satisfaction that I have survived the day of the accident.

Erica arrives just after 7:00 a.m. with giant cups of Dunkin' Donuts coffee and several chocolate honey-dipped dough-nuts, my favorite naughty breakfast. After we've eaten, Mom calls my stepfather, Charlie, while Erica escorts me to the unit's only shower, a few steps down the hall. Light-headed and unsteady, I hold her arm as we walk. Once inside the yellow-tiled, curtainless room, complete with plastic guest chair, she helps me remove my hospital gown, then watches protectively as I fumble in excruciatingly slow motion with the faucets and soap, trying to lather and rinse all six feet of me while maintaining balance and keeping my plastic-wrapped forearm elevated. Inept and embarrassed, I imagine I know how my eighty-year-old grandmother felt when she unexpect-edly needed me to haul her withered body out of the tub one time when I visited her during high school. Like a male doctor performing a breast exam, Erica chats about superficial topics—the cold front moving in, what she'll make for dinner that night—in a vain attempt to defuse the awkwardness of the situation.

Dad arrives just after Erica and I return to the room. "Hey, folks! How's everyone doing?" As Mom gingerly extricates my arm from the plastic sheath I've worn in the shower and Erica styles my hair into a French twist, Dad, a talented amateur photographer, darts around us snapping candid black-and-white photos with his professionally outfitted digital camera. His seemingly blithe attitude clearly annoys Mom, but I know the camera gives him a needed sense of purpose in this most disturbingly uncontrollable situation, and that the resulting images will be a testament to his watchfulness.

Around 11:00 a.m. Dr. Matthews, one of Dr. Vargas's team members, comes to discharge me. "You look ready to go," he says, flipping and signing pages on his clipboard.

"Was it the updo or the lip gloss that tipped you off?" I say. He laughs, then instructs me to return for a checkup in one week—or immediately if my fingers turn blue, indicating insufficient blood flow to the hand—and cautions me against moving the muscles of my hand, as the repaired tendons will be at risk of rupture for six weeks or so.

As Erica helps me wind myself up in a couple of wool wraps she's brought, a coat sleeve being too narrow to fit over my bulky dressing, she informs me she'll be taking me to her Upper East Side one-bedroom apartment to stay for a while. Though I haven't thought about where I'll go from the hospital, the plan surprises me because Erica, an exacting person, does not share personal space comfortably. However, my apartment lacks a functioning toilet, and the difficulty of my morning's ablutions have made it clear I can't care for myself, so I appreciate her foresight and sensitivity.

At her apartment that afternoon, Erica ushers me straight

to her inviting, pillow-laden bed for a nap. While she doles out my prescribed cocktail of pain medication, anti-inflammatories, and antibiotics onto the bedside table, I try to find a comfortable position for sleeping with the outsize foam elbow rest the nurses have supplied to keep my hand elevated, which we have dubbed "The Guggenheim" for the thick straps that encircle it, like the floors winding around the famous New York museum.

Dad kisses me goodbye before catching a train back to Rhode Island with Kate. "You can do this, kid. I'll call you every day," he promises. I suspect they are cutting their stay short to give Mom space, since she plans to stay in town awhile to help Erica care for me, and Erica will take some time off from work to do so. Neither Mom nor Erica circumscribes the scope of her assistance with specific dates, and I can't think far enough ahead to see a problem with that.

After my nap, Erica, Mom, and I have an evening snack, then Mom leaves for her hotel and Erica and I retire early to her bed. Every three hours and forty-five minutes throughout the night my burning hand awakens me, and assisted by Erica, who wakes the instant she feels my body shift on the mattress, I take another couple of pills to assuage the pain. Between doses, I sleep fitfully and dream of violence. Dining out with friends in one dream, I am disgusted but not surprised to find the restaurant's bathroom strewn with severed limbs and smeared with layers of blood, both fresh and dried. "So *this* is how it's going to be," I mutter, eyeing the filthy toilet seat.

6

.....

Big-Wave Surfing: Replanting a Partially Amputated Hand

I credit my Brooklyn posse—four close girlfriends I'd met singing in a local choir—with helping me piece together my recollections of the accident and its early aftermath, which they did over an evening of gently persistent questioning shortly after I moved back into my apartment. But my surgery was a big blank page in the story that took months of research, and several interviews with Dr. Vargas, to fill.

Walking into the operating room for my surgery, I learned, Dr. Vargas had to sweep a host of competing thoughts out of his mind to get into "the zone" for the event. As chief resident of Bellevue's hand-surgery team, a rotating position held by sixth-year plastic surgery residents, his responsibilities were diverse and consuming.

Beginning at seven o'clock each morning he checked on postoperative hand patients recovering in the wards, while engaging the junior residents accompanying him in instructive dialogue about each case. From midafternoon until the day's slate was clean, he performed and supervised hand surgeries, sometimes running back and forth between operating rooms when the volume and severity of cases demanded concurrent procedures. Two mornings per week he followed up with discharged patients at Bellevue's outpatient clinic; and during any of these activities, he could be summoned to the emergency department or wards to advise staff on hand-trauma cases—just as he had been for mine.

The job would be demanding in any large hospital, but it could be crushing at Bellevue, a major referral center for highly complex medical problems, including acute trauma. As a patient and later a volunteer there myself, I saw reattached fingers that had been severed by circular saws, machetes, and industrial equipment; hands shot through by guns and run over by trucks; arms smashed by construction materials and degloved in traffic accidents. Bellevue staff saw more and worse.

Dr. Vargas was well prepared for the job, having performed hundreds of relevant procedures during his residency to date. But my spaghetti wrist was a big deal, even at Bellevue, even for the chief. While the hand-surgery team repaired severed tendons, nerves, and blood vessels every day, they rarely confronted so many severed structures in a single patient, especially in the dominant hand of a person with many years yet to live and earn.

The severed radial artery—the most alarming part of the injury from my perspective—actually posed the least threat to my well-being going into the surgery, since I'd stopped its bleeding in my apartment, and Dr. Vargas had confirmed that my hand received adequate blood flow without it.

But my hand's entire ability to sense, grasp, and manipulate objects depended upon the combined function of the other severed structures: the median nerve, which drives motor and sensory function for most of the hand, and the flexor tendons, which enable the hand's digits to curl in toward the palm. In its injured state, my hand was just a big, floppy fork to push things around with, or a weird, warm paperweight to keep stuff from blowing away.

Restoration of any function at all would require a three-legged relay. First, Dr. Vargas would have to bring and stitch the stumps of the severed structures together, because they wouldn't otherwise reconnect. Then nature would have to permanently knit them in place and grow an extension of the median nerve to replace the severed stretch. And with an occupational therapist's help, I'd have to spend hundreds of hours teaching my "replanted" hand how to move again. Even if all that went well, my hand would never be "good as new." But we could hope that I'd recover sufficient strength, range of motion, and sensation in the hand to continue living much as I had before the accident.

To ace his part of the relay, Dr. Vargas needed tendon stumps with edges strong and straight enough to hold stitches.

If they'd been torn or crushed in the explosion, he'd have to consider more complicated procedures for restoring function to my hand, with poorer chances of success. Their condition was undiscernible to the naked eye, however. Until he could explore them under strong magnification in the operating room, he wouldn't know whether the odds of an optimal outcome ran for or against me.

If Dr. Vargas and I had met as healer and patient at various earlier points in history, we'd have much more to worry about than just my future hand function. At the most basic level, modern surgery—meaning surgery that is safe, effective, and humane—depends on the ability to control blood flow, because too much bleeding will kill a patient quickly, and too little blood to limbs or organs will maim or kill a patient slowly. It depends upon a thorough understanding of human anatomy—of what's what, how it works with everything else to produce a result, and how to handle different tissue types least invasively—so that a surgeon can devise a repair strategy that will help, not harm.

Modern surgery depends on the ability to control patients' pain and level of consciousness—not only to keep patients comfortable, but also to keep them perfectly still, so that surgeons can accurately "throw" the smallest of sutures within the smallest of structures. And it depends on the ability to prevent and treat infection, lest surgeons' best efforts in the operating room be bested later by the pernicious bacteria constantly seeking human hosts in which to breed and feed.

We take this body of knowledge and capability for granted today, but it emerged in literally painful fits and starts over millennia, and only became (more or less) complete and pervasive in Western medical practice in the twentieth century, when antibiotics became widely available. Why so long and late? Of course, there's the fact that innovation requires discovery, discovery involves luck, and luck (tragically contrary to idiom) doesn't always favor the prepared, even if they're trying to save lives. But innumerable other, interconnected reasons exist; and a few among them stand out.

For one, excepting a relatively brief heyday in ancient Alexandria, cultural and religious objections to human cadaveric dissection, as well as a lack of appreciation for its value in medical education, limited its practice until the thirteenth and fourteenth centuries. Even then, misconceptions of human anatomy based on animal dissection (dogs, pigs, and monkeys being the preferred models) persisted until the mid-sixteenth century, when physician Andreas Vesalius exposed them through closely observed human dissection, leading to its broad recognition as an essential teaching tool.

Further, lacking modern methods of observation and experimentation, surgeons often couldn't conclusively determine whether the interventions they performed worked or not. Thus their patients suffered mightily while surgeons inflicted, and debated the theoretical merits of, deadly treatments like blood-letting, and promoting "laudable pus" in a wound.

Even when surgeons did land on an effective intervention, factors that still frustrate the medical profession today might bedevil its broad adoption. Perhaps it wasn't communicated in a channel or language accessible to a specific population of practitioners. Or surgeons rejected it because the evidence in its favor, however sound, contradicted their personal experience or beliefs. And then, some effective interventions just mysteriously slipped out of practice, only to resurface decades or centuries later.

But neither ignorance nor the agony and mortal peril of their patients tempered the astonishing ambition of Dr. Vargas's professional ancestors. In prehistoric times, they bored holes into each other's heads—whether for medical or ritualistic purposes, we'll never know. In ancient times they amputated limbs, removed bladder stones, and reconstructed leprosy-ravaged noses. They sewed up lacerated nerves and intestines in the Middle Ages, and repaired aneurysms during the Renaissance. And in a nineteenth-century coup de non-grâce, a team of them in France performed a mastectomy on novelist Fanny Burney. *Sans* anesthetic.

Several body parts tingle in sympathetic offense as I type up these examples, and I wonder which current medical practices will horrify us in another quarter century—when, no doubt, I'll enjoy the convenience of performing my own hip replacement at home with the help of my robotic canine companion. But in fairness to those whose cringeworthy work I've highlighted, historical accounts suggest that they sometimes achieved their objectives, sometimes without killing their patients (at the risk of splitting hairs, I must point out that amputating a leg, and preventing the amputee's death by hemorrhage or infection, are two different things). Burney's was one such case, and she wrote an account of the ordeal, though you'll want to give it a pass if you had any trouble stomaching the first chapter of this book.

Also, medicine cannot advance without ethical experimentation and practice. Given I had no choice but to join the living objects of such endeavors, then, I'm ecstatic to have done so in an era when my surgical team knew how to keep me alive and comfortable during the procedure, and give me the best shot at functional recovery that the latest scientific evidence could afford.

By the time my ER bed and I rolled into the operating room on Bellevue's eleventh floor, the party in my honor was in full swing. A generous handful of nurses and doctors busied themselves in various corners of the bright, cold space, laying out instruments and supplies and setting up equipment. They had worked together on numerous occasions, and most had trained in the particulars of hand surgery related to their roles, so they knew the procedure I'd undergo and each other's working preferences well.

After I'd awkwardly scooched onto the operating table from the rolling bed, the scrub nurse secured my outstretched right arm to a slim extension of the table. Dr. Vargas and his assisting resident, Dr. Matthews, already sat facing each other on either side of the extension—Dr. Vargas's left side to my right—and began quietly conferring and gesturing around my wrist.

The anesthesiologist started an IV opiate in my left arm and, once I'd slipped out of consciousness seconds later, worked a breathing tube down my trachea. Then she began pumping an anesthetic gas through it, which would keep me unconscious and still (paralyzed, actually, but I'll get to that in chapter 8) for the duration of the procedure. In the meantime, the scrub nurse placed a screen at my right shoulder, to separate the sterile operating field (my arm) from the non-sterile anesthesia equipment on the other side of my body, then draped a sterile blue sheet over the screen, my head, and the rest of my body, leaving my arm exposed. Finally, the team took their places for the main event.

"You can't fix a watch in a bottle of ink," said Sterling Bunnell, the granddaddy of American hand surgery, in the days of pocket watches and fountain pens. In other words, even the smallest traces of blood could obscure the minute structures Dr. Vargas needed to work on during the surgery. Before he could begin, then, he and Dr. Matthews needed to eliminate any blood remaining in the wound and ensure none would seep back in while they operated. They accomplished this through a procedure that goes by the deliciously disgusting term *exsanguination.*

First, they tightly wrapped a long, elasticized bandage from my fingertips to my bicep, progressively squeezing all the blood in the limb back into my trunk, like toothpaste out of a tube. To keep it there, they inflated a tourniquet cuff on my bicep, applying just enough pressure to close the vessels supplying the limb, but not so much as to damage the nerves there. Finally, they removed the bandage to expose the sutured wound.

My arm could do without blood for a while. But starved of it too long and cells would begin to die, threatening extensive tissue loss and gangrene. To stay well clear of that point, Dr. Vargas needed to complete the procedure in three hours— four at the absolute maximum. If he couldn't finish in that time frame, they'd have to deflate the cuff to allow my arm to refill with blood; then once it had enjoyed a good feeding, exsanguinate it all over again. He set a timer on the inflated cuff for ninety minutes to remind them of the halfway point, sat down, and turned again to my wrist.

According to Dr. Vargas's written report of the operation, he next "appreciated" the wound. I like to imagine him slowly shaking his head, muttering, "Man, that is *one great wound.*" But really, he was just considering whether he'd need to extend the laceration to create more room in which to work. Which he didn't. Instead, he removed the stitches placed in the ER, donned glasses fitted with magnifying loops, tied off the artery stumps with silk thread, and set about locating each tendon in my wrist, noting which remained, which had been cut, which could be fixed—and how, given the condition of their stumps.

Because tendons are always under a bit of tension, like a slightly taut rubber band, they retract into opposite sides of a wound when severed. This made finding the stumps a sort of macabre Easter egg hunt. To locate those on the hand side of the wound, Dr. Vargas crimped and wiggled my fingers one at a time until the stumps popped back into the wound, tricked into acting as if they'd been pulled there by the muscles in the forearm to which they'd formerly been attached. To locate the stumps on the arm side of the wound, where mechanical manipulation of the tendons isn't possible, he used forceps to carefully excavate along the path he knew that each tendon followed up the forearm.

Upon discovery, he marked each stump with a suture, then listed the name of the tendon it belonged to with a sterile pen on the margin of the blue sterile sheet draping my body . . . which is not as creepy as it sounds. Surgeons write on blue sheets all the time, because notepads compromise a sterile environment. The blue sheet list thus became the surgical plan: reconnect twelve tendon stumps, then two nerve stumps. Matching stumps for one other transected tendon couldn't be found without causing more damage, but those that could were firm, and cleanly cut (well done, toilet!). Dr. Vargas would be able to stitch each to its original mate, sparing me the paw he'd warned of in our first meeting.

While this wouldn't be a complex, puzzle-solving kind of

surgery, like constructing an opposable thumb from a toe, it would be tricky, unforgiving work. Tendons are strong but slippery, and they are small at the wrist, about the width and shape of two pieces of linguine, stacked. And while the median nerve at the wrist is much thicker than the tendons there, it's laughably fragile—like overcooked pasta wrapped in wet toilet paper, as Dr. Vargas later described it to me. He would have to precisely place many tiny stitches into these fussy structures, without damaging them. Moreover, because the hand's numerous parts are so highly integrated, even a small error or complication during the surgery could significantly impair my functional recovery. "Big-wave surfing," Dr. Vargas called the procedure. You have to get it right, or the consequences are dire.

He and the team knew their performance over the next several hours would indelibly influence how I lived the rest of my life, so the mood in the room was sober. But it was also focused, keen. After all, they'd spent years training for this kind of work. To the peppy white noise of '80s tunes playing softly on the operating room radio, Dr. Vargas reached for his forceps and dove in.

Responding to my machine-gun spray of questions about the procedure in a later checkup, Dr. Vargas could have discouraged my burning curiosity—which, after all, could only deepen a resident's chronic time deficit. Instead, he tossed accelerant on it by recommending "the book that all the big surgeons give their protégés," which I promptly ordered from Amazon.

A long, rapturous, and meticulously researched stroll through the evolution of reconstructive surgery, *The Healing Hand: Man and Wound in the Ancient World* gripped me throughout with its lucid prose, copious and uncommon visuals, and bone-dry wit (trust me). It transformed my medical science research from mere fact-finding about my injury and repair into a deeply satisfying end in itself, permeated with the joy of discovery and understanding, deepening my appreciation for my body, and giving me a powerful new lens through which to perceive common human experience.

Greedily consuming the book, I was struck by just how much the life-improving practice of surgery owes to the life-taking practice of war. Weapons innovation drives medical innovation, and apparently has since a hominin first planted an antelope femur in a neighbor's skull, prompting another neighbor to attempt the aforementioned hole-boring treatment (called *trepanation*, in case you want to watch some do-it-yourself evangelists effuse about it on YouTube). Thus, as found cudgels gave way to slingshots and arrows, then progressively to cannons, muskets, machine guns, and improvised explosive devices, ancient healers and their professional descendants have scrambled to develop effective means of managing the increasingly devastating wounds wrought.

Sometimes they've succeeded, often while practicing in militaries during wartime, or as a result of that experience.

That's partly due to the central tragedy of war—the creation of a large number and diversity of casualties—which offers surgeons extensive opportunity to trial, refine, and teach new approaches to care, on patients young and otherwise fit enough to stand a chance of responding well to them.

But medical innovation needs more than opportunity to flourish, and war has often enabled it in other important ways, aggregating multidisciplinary medical experts, skilled supporting staff, and cutting-edge equipment and technology, and focusing the lot on collaborative resolution of some of the toughest medical and care-delivery problems in an era. Combined with the urgent need to return wounded soldiers to combat fitness, which gives personnel a mandate to challenge entrenched practices, these conditions create an innovation engine that's difficult to replicate in ordinary circumstances. Modern hospital hygiene and sanitation protocols; the tourniquet and the ambulance; and numerous surgical techniques developed in this engine, as did the specialty of hand surgery.

Through the early decades of the twentieth century, good surgical solutions for many hand problems had yet to be identified. Further, most surgeons didn't know existing best practices for reconstructing severely damaged hands, so they usually left them that way. On rare occasions when hand reconstruction was attempted, specialist surgeons divvied the job up by tissue type, with plastic, orthopedic, and neurosurgeons tackling damaged skin, bones, and peripheral nerves, respectively, and worked in uncommunicating succession, without considering what the functional outcome of their collective efforts would, or should, be.

As a result, hand parts made whole didn't always work as a whole: Fractured fingers healed unable to oppose the thumb. Skin grafts lacked the slack to stretch over the knuckles of a closing hand. Poorly repaired nerves rendered otherwise-sound hands immobile. Disabling impairments were common.

In the US, where hand surgery professionalized somewhat earlier than in other Western countries, a smattering of surgeons rejected this status quo, including the aforementioned Bunnell. Unlike their mainstream colleagues, who viewed the hand as a collection of independent parts, they recognized the hand as a mobile system beginning in the arm, comprising numerous structures, and quickened by the nervous system. And they believed that maimed hands *could* be salvaged, if reconstruction strategies prioritized function of the hand system, rather than simply the integrity of its parts.

This "systems view" illuminated new possibilities for addressing previously insoluble hand problems, and following World War I, these pioneering surgeons worked independently to explore and develop them. It also highlighted the need for a new kind of surgical specialist—one who would take full responsibility for the overall function of a reconstructed hand system and could skillfully operate on all tissue types in order to maximize it.

The innovation engine revved up by World War II enabled the creation of that specialist job in the US. Compared to World War I, more devastating weapons, better war-zone trauma care, newly available antibiotics, and faster evacuation to well-equipped stateside hospitals in World War II meant that more soldiers were surviving with more severe injuries than in the prior conflict. Injuries mostly involved the extremities, very often the hand. Determined to avoid the manpower losses suffered in World War I due to incapacitating hand injuries, the US Army invested heavily in transforming treatment of the combat-injured hand, relying on the pioneering surgeons, and Bunnell in particular, to develop and implement the strategy for doing so.

Toward this end, the pioneers set up services in hospitals across the US dedicated to treatment of patients who required "formidable reconstruction of the hand" (as did I, according to their criteria). They defined rigorous qualifications for the new hand specialty, including "ingenuity" and a talent for teaching, on top of the already big ask of plastic, orthopedic, *and* neurosurgical skills. They trained a cohort of surgeons to meet them, led by Bunnell. And keen to embed their knowledge in common medical practice after World War II, they set up a professional association that still defines the specialty's US training and certification requirements, and facilitates the exchange of knowledge with colleagues abroad.

Today's hand-surgery pioneers are conducting military-funded research to improve outcomes for the steady flow of hand-injured enlistees and civilians created by armed conflicts. Thus, the vicious-virtuous circle of war and innovation persists, and Dr. Vargas could address my devastating injury with state-of-the-art techniques, on half a day's notice, in a civilian hospital. And thus, my uneasy gratitude for good fortune born of violence.

In the safety of the Bellevue operating room, scar tissue was Dr. Vargas's biggest enemy. Or frenemy, really, because it's the body's main mechanism for healing. A wound anywhere in the body causes tissue cell damage, hence a gap in healthy tissue that must be filled in order to restore function. In an elegant solution to this problem, the damaged cells release chemicals that trigger generation of healthy replacements. But the body doesn't replace the former with their own kind; it does so with its all-purpose adhesive, scar tissue. Soft but strong and stretchy, scar tissue is ace for any human DIY repair job, from smoothing over a skinned knee to knitting up a torn ligament.

What's the problem? While generated at the wound site, scar tissue doesn't stay there. Left to its nature, it indiscriminately oozes into the spaces in and around any other tissue it encounters, like foam insulation injected into a wall cavity, and sticks to it. And in excess or in the wrong place, it impedes function of the very structures it is designed to mend. Not so elegant.

The double-edged nature of scar tissue informs every aspect of hand repair: When you do it, which must be before scarring glues retracted tendon and nerve stumps to their accidental resting places in the hand and forearm. How you do it, with the most delicate instruments and fewest necessary stitches, because even a minuscule suture hole is just a wound waiting for scar tissue to fill and spill out of it. Scar tissue even determines whether you attempt repair at all, because sometimes its likely impact outweighs any potential functional gain from a procedure. As such, it demanded Dr. Vargas's consideration throughout the surgery, beginning with repair of the tendons.

Tendons are the boss of bones. As described in chapter 4, they're activated by the muscles they emerge from on one end, and they make the bones to which they're attached on the other assume whatever position the central nervous system commands. But like puppet strings, they can only pull, not push, their object. So whatever direction a bone needs to move in, there's a tendon to pull it that way.

In the hand, this means that when you make a fist, your flexor tendons pull the bones of your digits down and in toward your palm; and when you wave, your extensor tendons pull your digits out and away from your palm. And however you move your hand, tendons are gliding back and forth through tissue and over joints.

To give me the best shot at full range of motion, then, Dr. Vargas had to stitch my transected tendons together in a way that enabled gliding. Working stump pair by stump pair, he did so by checking that the tendons weren't twisted, and by aligning matching stumps on cross-section to preclude bulging edges. Then he used forceps to manipulate his needles—needles not threaded but seamlessly crimped to both ends of a plastic filament—in a clever stitch pattern that surgeons have been tinkering with since the 1970s.

Biting in and out of the stiff exterior and squishy interior of the tendon stumps, Dr. Vargas secured two strands of thread in each, so that their loose ends (four per stump) dangled into the juncture between paired stumps. He then pulled the eight dangling strands together and knotted them, bringing each pair of stumps together. And that was that: Dr. Vargas's best effort, aligned with best practices of the day, at a repair posing minimal risk of scarring, and strong enough to hold while I did gentle hand exercises to keep joints supple until the tendons fully healed.

The median-nerve repair required a very different approach from that of the tendons. A day or two after the accident, the median-nerve axons below the wound—which had died when severed from their cell bodies in or near the spinal cord—would disintegrate, leaving the nerve's outermost sheath intact. Hopefully, the live ends of the axons—those above the wound, thus still connected to their cell bodies—would regenerate, per another of humanity's magnificent survival programs that I'll explore more fully in chapter 12.

To reestablish their feedback loop with the central nervous system, regenerating axons would first need to cross the wound, and Dr. Vargas aimed to help them do so by reconnecting the stumps of the nerve sheath, thus forming a covered bridge over the wound. Next, the axons would need to reach their designated patches of tissue in the forearm and hand, with motor and sensory axons each terminating at different types of non-neuronal cells (which I'll generalize as "target cells"). Chances were slim that many axons would make the journey successfully. But almost certainly, none would if Dr. Vargas didn't execute a good nerve-sheath repair.

A good sheath repair begins with alignment of the sheath stumps on cross-section, so that regenerating motor axons might "stick to their lanes" and find motor target cells, and regenerating sensory axons might likewise find sensory target cells. If motor axons try to dock at sensory target cells and vice versa, well, that's like trying to plug an iPhone charger into an Android phone. No juice. To achieve alignment, Dr. Vargas would use the tiny, faint blood vessels running longitudinally through the sheath as landmarks in finding the correct orientation of stumps to each other, as if matching up the red stripes on a broken candy cane, but harder. Then he'd secure the stumps together with knots at six even intervals around the sheath's circumference.

Dr. Vargas did all this fine work looking through the lenses of a powerful standing microscope positioned over my wrist—sitting with elbows cradled by rests to help still his hands; using forceps to manipulate needles the length and curvature of an eyelash and no thicker; fingers barely moving; gently throwing stitches, pulling up slack, and knotting and clipping—until he'd finally crossed the last item off the long list of repairs on my blue sheet.

Three and a half hours after he began, Dr. Vargas deflated the tourniquet cuff to let my arm refill with blood, used an electric cautery to close some small vessels unlikely to clot on their own, and closed my wound for the last time. Then he raised my forearm off the table, took hold of my hand at the wrist joint, and carefully moved it back and forth.

In a hand with properly functioning tendons, the fingers

naturally fall into a cascade as the wrist moves forward, like Adam's in Michelangelo's Sistine Chapel painting of creation, and they form a loose fist as the wrist moves back, like babies' hands do when they sleep on their backs. And so did my fingers as Dr. Vargas moved my wrist. The repaired tendons had passed their first test. They could still rupture, axons could still fail to regrow, and scar tissue could still gum up the repaired structures. But the surgery, at least, had gone very well.

While Drs. Vargas and Matthews set my wrist and hand in a light plaster cast, the room came alive again as the rest of the team briskly cleaned, set up for the next surgery, and hurried out of the room. If they were hopeful or worried about the surgery or my future, they couldn't dwell on those feelings. They had to clear me from their minds and hearts so they could give the next patient their best, too. That was the job; for many, their calling.

However they felt about their work, to me it was an aligning of stars—of extraordinary knowledge, skill, and determination, wrung from sacrifice and compounded over centuries, finally available and summoned on my behalf at 3:00 p.m. on a Friday afternoon in 2006. And invested by the team in me, a stranger, with nothing expected in return, it was an act of compassion—of love, even—as healing as anything else that happened in the operating room that day.

7
.....

Under Water on the Upper East Side

The next six days pass indistinctly. Befuddled by medication and the lingering effects of trauma, I am perpetually exhausted and in pain, eat little, and have difficulty concentrating on stressful but necessary tasks that Mom and Erica can't execute for me, like handing work projects off to colleagues and submitting health insurance claims. I live underwater, swept along by a slow current past sights that used to be familiar—Erica's apartment, city sidewalks, the few close friends who visit—but look strange from my new perspective. Why aren't I in *my* home, going to *my* job every day? Didn't I used to be able to walk outside without fear of bodily harm? Have my friends ever wept for me before now? I observe, rather than participate in, this alien world.

Searching for a mental landmark that will help me find my bearings, I assess my situation for a similar challenge I've surmounted before, a requisite skill I'm confident I possess. I find none. Instead, I worry whether the searing pains in my hand signify life or decay, what it will take to wean myself from the powerful pain medication, how to tell my boss I don't know when I will return to work.

Most unsettling, I have no vision of the future. Will I be able to hold a pen and write? Or write but not type, or type but not without looking at the keys? Will I feel closer to loved ones, or lonelier for having had an experience they may never understand? Having been violently forced to confront my mortality, will I find "normal" life a blessing, or stupid and superficial? Overwhelmed by these unanswerable questions, I sorely feel the lack of a mentor to spot me through my trial.

One night as I lie in bed trying to fall asleep, I remember that a business school classmate, Scott, survived a terrible accident two years prior. We're not close, so I only learned about it through a chance meeting with him at our class reunion a few months ago.

At the time, I hadn't fully grasped his explanation of the damage done to his hand and arm, which looked normal to the untrained eye, only that it had been extensive. Now, replaying the hazy fragments of conversation I can retrieve from memory, I realize that we must have suffered similar injuries. If so, he could surely tell me something of what to expect from my body in the near future.

I go to the living room, kneel in front of the side table where Erica keeps her laptop, and flip it open. It's password protected, so I have to get creative to bring up the password prompt, pressing the Delete key with a pencil I clench between my teeth, while holding down the Ctrl and Alt keys with two fingers of my left hand. Success! I spit out the pencil and enter the password Erica has written for me on a Post-it note stuck to the desk. Once I've tracked down Scott's email address on our school's alumni website, I open up a new email message, paste the address in, awkwardly type a brief note, and compose a subject line I hope will cut through any clutter in his inbox: *Advice and encouragement for a fellow hand-injury sufferer?* Then I go back to bed, spent but hopeful.

The next morning, I see that Scott has already responded, offering warm wishes and help. He proposes calling me from his home in London as soon as our schedules jibe, which turns out to be a few days later.

"I have lots of good, practical advice for you," he begins. "But first, I have to tell you something. And you're going to think I'm crazy for saying this, but someday you'll know it's true." He pauses. "You're *lucky* this happened to you."

Like so many words of late, these make no sense. I do feel lucky that the ballistic shard of porcelain slashed my wrist instead of, say, piercing my jugular vein and ensuring a quick, ignoble death in a blood-soaked negligee. But the suggestion that the accident has been a *good thing* . . . well, that strikes me as pretty radical. Then again, flying high on hydrocodone, I lack the mental agility to wrap my head around subtle concepts, so maybe I'm missing his point.

"Uh, OK. Why's that?" I ask cautiously.

"Because you're going to learn and experience things that you couldn't any other way," he replies. "Amazing, *wonderful* things that most people go their whole lives without knowing."

I can't deny the truth in the cliché that tough experiences often teach useful lessons. But at that moment, in bed and bone-tired at 7:00 p.m. because I can't stay awake for more than three hours at a stretch, contemplating my total loss of independence, ambition, and ability to make the most basic decisions about my immediate future, I still can't imagine what benefits the accident might yield that could possibly justify the pain, anxiety, and dilemmas it has caused. It just feels like a brutal exercise in grit. But I want to believe it will prove as . . . worthwhile . . . as Scott has predicted, so I promise to reconsider that possibility when I'm feeling stronger.

Turning to the subject of rehabilitation, Scott and I determine we've both suffered severe damage to tendons and nerves serving our hands, which threatens their long-term functionality. He tells me I can expect months of occupational therapy (OT), and predictably preaches the importance of adhering to the exercise regimen my occupational therapist will design for me. I don't expect his ensuing advice, however, which is essentially "Play doctor."

"Learn everything you can about the hand—the anatomy, mechanics, *everything*," he urges. "That way you know what the hand is *trying* to do in healing. Then when it reaches a big milestone, you can appreciate just how hard it worked to get there. And when it's progressing slowly or not at all, you understand why and won't be so demoralized."

I'm skeptical about the value of learning so much about my hand when the surgery has already taken place and I don't have any treatment decisions to make. But I need little excuse to indulge my curiosity and have no better ideas for coping at the moment. So I decide to trust Scott on this point, too, and hit the internet with resolve the next day.

I have my first chance to test the efficacy of Scott's prescription when I see Drs. Vargas and Matthews the following week for the postoperative checkup. Mom, Erica, and Charlie, who has flown in for a few days, come with me, and they crowd into the corners of the small clinic room like a celebrity security detail, while I perch myself on the end of the examination table. Dr. Matthews sits at the computer, ready to take notes.

Once Dr. Vargas has examined the surgical site and checked blood circulation in my hand, I ask some of the many questions I've prepared. Which of the severed structures did the surgeons repair in the surgery? Six of the seven tendons, and the sheath of the nerve. What about the artery? They tied it off. Blood flow to my hand was sufficient without it. Why has the skin on the palm of my hand become disgustingly thick, scaly, and flaky? One reason could be because the cut nerve used to moderate the hand's temperature by activating sweat glands in the skin. Now that it can't, those glands are inactive, and the skin has dried out for lack of moisture. It will return to normal once the nerve grows back. Will I be able to type again? Maybe, but probably not without looking at the keys, because I won't be able to feel them. Will I be able to play violin? Had I played violin before? A long time ago, but I always hoped to get back to it. Again maybe, if I can do it without being able to feel the bow.

The surgeons answer my questions thoroughly, if dryly. But their tone is lighter than that of our previous interviews, for while the situation remains serious, the crisis has passed. Dr. Vargas reinforces that the surgery went well, inspiring cautious confidence I will regain some basic nerve sensibility and individual finger motion. He qualifies his positive assessment of my status, cautioning, "Never say 'never,' never say 'always,' they teach us," but even his well-practiced poker face doesn't completely disguise some cheer.

Finally, I tell Dr. Vargas I am having difficulty conveying the severity of my injury to people who can't see it for themselves. The phrase "cut to the bone" too often elicits the response "But they stitched you up, right?" as if the surgery were the end of the story.

"Can you give me some analogy that anyone could relate to?" I ask. "Like, how serious is my injury on a scale from, say, planned C-section to emergency coronary bypass?"

Dr. Vargas regards me with cocked head and furrowed brow as I admit particular concern that my boss and colleagues understand the justification for the indefinite medical leave for which I'm applying.

"Tell them it's a *partial amputation*," he snaps. "See if they understand *that*."

I tuck my list of questions back into my bag. Our business concluded, Dr. Vargas bolts toward the door so quickly I have to call out, "Wait, stop!" He turns, eyebrows ever so slightly arched, and takes a couple of steps back into the room. "This is the thank-you portion of our meeting," I explain.

He leans up against the doorframe, looking mildly impatient but curious; Dr. Matthews turns from his post-appointment documentation at the computer to listen. I warmly express my gratitude for the care the surgeons and their colleagues have provided: Miles, who held my hand during the ambulance ride to the hospital; Dr. Goldstein, who kept me from being sent home to await surgery; the one nurse who removed a bloody ring from my swelling fingers and washed it before stowing for safekeeping; the other who told me I was brave; the anesthesiologist whose gallows humor kept me laughing right up to the moment she put me under.

"This is a once-in-a-lifetime ordeal for *me*," I say, pausing to steady my voice, "but you do what you've done for me every day, for so many others. I just hope you know the incredible impact you have on your patients' lives. I'll never forget it."

The surgeons look down momentarily, fiddling with papers, shifting their feet. "Well . . . we . . . like our jobs," Dr. Vargas finally replies. As my family and I say goodbye to Dr. Matthews, who has turned back to the computer, Dr. Vargas lingers at the doorway. On our way out I hand him a card, laboriously scratched out in my unpracticed left hand, and ask him to show it to all the people I've mentioned. Wordlessly taking my left hand in both of his, he holds it for several seconds and stares at me.

Before leaving the hospital, I have to go to the hand-splinting room down the hall to meet my occupational therapist, Beth. So Erica accompanies me there and takes a seat outside, while Mom and Charlie head back to their hotel. Beth beckons me to sit down and prop my right elbow up on a small table resembling the manicure stations in a nail salon.

As far as my murky understanding goes, her job is not only to get my hand moving again, but to help me regain the ability to perform essential activities like eating, dressing, and typing. Sitting opposite me now, she carefully clips the plastered bandage off my hand and forearm with a pair of surgical shears. Bruised yellow-green, swollen several glove sizes, and studded with scores of prickly black stitches that trek across the blood-traced wound like a parade of spiders, the hand is difficult to recognize as my own, or as having the potential ever to be useful again. It looks grotesque and menacing, yet naked and imperiled, an infant born desperately premature. Acquainting myself with my new hand, I feel a mixture of revulsion and affection, like the heroine of *Rosemary's Baby* viewing her demonic progeny for the first time.

"Wow, it looks *great!*" Beth says, gently turning my wrist back and forth. "The wound's knitting well. There's a lot of swelling, but that's totally normal, we can work on that. How long's it been, just a week?" With her smooth skin, Puma sneakers, and numerous ear piercings, she can't be more than twenty-five, but she speaks with the reassuring confidence of one who has seen limbs and lives much more grievously damaged than mine.

Beth spends the next thirty minutes custom-fitting me with a removable hard-plastic splint that will hold my hand in a "neutral" position—fingers aligned and bent ninety degrees to palm, thumb outstretched forty-five degrees from palm—that puts no strain on the healing tendons. She tells me to wash the splint every day in warm, soapy water. "Otherwise it's going to get *really* stinky *really* fast!"

Finally, she assigns exercises to keep my joints supple for the next six weeks, during which I won't be able to exert my healing flexor tendons. These entail using my left hand to crimp the fingers of my right hand down to my palm, then slowly allowing the right fingers to extend back to the neutral position on their own. "Let's say, ten reps of these three times a day. It's *really* important that you do them all, or your hand will turn into a block of wood and it'll be a lot harder to get good movement back," she warns with the tough-love tone of a big sister. Obviously she doesn't know my work ethic yet. She sends me off cheerily, instructing me to return the following Tuesday to begin our regimen in earnest. I leave the hospital excited to begin participating in my recovery.

Returning to Erica's apartment, she and I find Mom installed in the living room behind the A-section of the *New*

York Times. I head straight to the sofa for a nap, and Erica briefly sits at the dining room table to finish my medical leave application, then goes to the kitchen to bake a pan of brownies. Concerned about my uncharacteristically poor appetite, she has tested the appeal of various dishes over the past week, finding that only brownies or scrambled eggs drizzled in truffle oil consistently induce me to eat.

Half-awake a little later, I hear Mom and Erica whispering sharply, apparently disagreeing over the priority of the afternoon's care tasks—getting a prescription filled, buying a big sweatshirt whose right arm I can push my splint through, others I can't quite make out. It's unusual for them not to get along; the stress of the whole situation is obviously getting to them, too. I hope it's "only" that, anyway. My internist has told us that my trauma could cause my loved ones to reexperience distress related to adverse events in their own lives. The tension soon eases, though, and after Mom has collected my medication, we all cozy up on the couch to watch British comedies on BBC America, a shared favorite indulgence.

The next day the building management company calls to tell me that my bathroom has finally been repaired. At dinner that night, I am attempting to wind strands of pesto pasta around the fork in my left hand when Erica blurts out, "Hey, you guys can go to Becca's apartment now, right? Because I . . . really need to get my life back." I'm stunned. I didn't think I'd be staying with Erica for months, but I certainly hadn't expected to leave after just over a week. I'm not ready to do without her help, and I fight the urge to leap out of my seat and yell, "I want my life back, too, but it'll never be the same, and I don't even know how I'm going to get through the next week!" Instead I look down at my plate, blinking rapidly to stem welling tears, and respond, "Yeah, we can go in a couple days." Erica has done all she can. It's time to move on.

8

.....

With Respect to Pain:
How It Helps and Works

Get two taps into any mindfulness meditation app, and you're bound to encounter the expression "Pain is inevitable, suffering is optional." Rooted in Buddhist philosophy, it means that while we can't escape hurtful experiences, we can learn to respond to them in a way that makes them more bearable. As I explored and eventually embraced its ancient insight, I realized how well it aligns with contemporary science's understanding of pain resulting from physical injury.

In concept, such pain is an ugly monolith: solid and uniformly bad, something always to fear, avoid, assuage. But examining the actual experience of it, we find it comprises both physical and emotional effects, varies widely in quality and intensity, and can flicker on and off. It also teaches us to avoid danger and prompts us to care for ourselves and others— healthy and compassionate impulses, however unpleasant their genesis.

Given these observations, the neural underpinnings of pain make sense. Imagine that you accidentally kick the leg of your bed while shuffling to the bathroom in the middle of the night, breaking the little toe on your right foot. Which I have done, twice. You feel a short, sharp pain in the toe and, a couple of ticks later, a diffuse, burning sensation engulfing the whole top-right corner of your foot. Then, if you are like me, you cuss vigorously at the unpleasantness while hobbling to the kitchen for a bag of frozen peas to remedy it.

Both waves of physical pain, the sharp and the burning, are triggered by nociceptors, a class of sensory neuron that detects tissue damage and potentially harmful levels of heat, cold, force, and/or chemical irritation. Detecting the impact of your toe-bed collision, nociceptors send data about it into the central nervous system, where its processing causes automatic with-drawal of your foot from the bed and assessment of the event's existential significance to you. At some point during all this activity, by means shrouded in the mysteries of consciousness, you become aware that *you* are experiencing the sensation that you have learned to call "pain," and you are not happy about it.

Why do the two waves of pain feel different? Part of the answer lies in how data collected by different nociceptors travels to, and through, your brain. Some data races toward it through roomy, insulated sensory axons at up to 150 miles per hour. It arrives before any other neural news of your mishap, thus triggering the first wave of pain. And you feel that pain clearly concentrated in your toe because the data is processed in the brain by the somatosensory cortex, which precisely analyzes its source in the body. This precision is essential because the purpose of that first wave of pain is to enable your removal from immediate danger, and the central nervous system needs to know exactly which part of you is endangered in order to do that.

Other nociceptor data travels through narrow, uninsulated sensory axons at the pokey pace of about two miles per hour, so the pain it triggers blossoms after the first wave, the length of delay positively correlated with the distance between the data's source and the brain. This second wave of pain covers more territory than the first because the parts of the brain that initially process the slow nociceptor data don't precisely localize its source in the body. They don't need to, as the second wave's purpose is to prevent further injury by motivating you to protect the toe by a wide margin, for instance by keeping pressure off the right part of your foot while walking.

While the first wave of pain lasts mere seconds, the second persists for minutes or hours. And, alas, you're not off the hook even then, because your broken toe also leads to *inflammatory pain*. This takes hold when your immune system releases a deluge of chemicals into the injured area to combat pathogens that may have entered the body there, and to initiate repair of damaged tissue. These chemicals cause the warmth, redness, and swelling characteristic of inflammation, and some of them activate nociceptors, which in turn trigger a burning pain much like the second wave.

Inflammatory pain differs from acute pain in several important ways, however. It is exacerbated by normally innocuous stimuli (like light touch or mild heat), because the body's immune response lowers the activation thresholds of some nociceptors. It spreads more broadly, as nociceptors firing in the area of injury set off those in adjacent, healthy tissue. And it persists for days or even weeks, in part because the nociceptors involved don't simply react to their environment. They change it by releasing chemicals back into the injured area, which assist in the healing process but also help sustain the very conditions that cause them to trigger pain in the first place. Oh, the costs of your midnight trip to the bathroom! But in making you reluctant to touch or burden the affected area, inflammatory pain performs the valuable function of keeping your toe safe until it has fully healed.

Along with their physical manifestations, both acute and inflammatory pain bring a liberal lacing of unpleasant emotion—pain's power to anger, worry, sadden, and demoralize us. This is the kind of suffering to which the popular meditation expression refers, and its cleverness in this context lies in the insight that the emotional and physical aspects of pain may seem completely inseparable, but they are not. If we pay very close attention, we can discern between them.

You can try, right now. Close your eyes and sit or stand as still as you can. Scan your body for some unpleasant sensation—sore feet, backache, period cramps, anything. If none presents itself, yet you're keen to experiment, flex one of your biceps and give yourself a hearty pinch on the top of it. Now concentrate on the resulting sensation for a minute. Can you describe its location, quality, consistency, or intensity?

Next, tune in to your mental state. Can you discern a particular attitude toward the sensation—perhaps annoyance, curiosity, or indifference? If you can answer both these questions in the affirmative, you have perceived the distinction that exists between what we feel and how we feel about it, which is also reflected in the distinct ingredients and processes by which the brain creates our sensations and emotions.

Why bother? Because we can sometimes exploit these distinctions to our relief when pain arises. Like all our emotions, those accompanying painful sensations are the product of various nonemotional ingredients, including bodily feedback (such as nociceptor signals), our attention to particular sensory stimuli (that burning, broken toe), and facts and personal history stored in memory that shape how we interpret the significance of a given situation. By consciously tweaking some of these, we can alter the quality of our emotions.

Many of us do this intuitively, perhaps turning our attention from a sore muscle to a pleasantly engaging conversation, or reflecting on the long-term health benefits enabled by an unavoidable surgery, instead of dwelling on normal postoperative pain. Such tactics may have little impact on the physical experience of pain, and they are no substitute for its professional, evidence-based treatment, where appropriate. But they can lessen pain's overall burden by reducing the unpleasantness of its emotional component, and that's a real mitzvah in our unavoidably painful lives.

Every one of us experiences pain differently, and would, even in the impossible event that we sustained the exact same injury. Biological factors like genes and health status contribute to the differences, as do psychological and environmental factors like mood and cultural beliefs about the meaning of pain and "appropriate" responses to it. The variability of the pain experience, and the fact that an individual's experience cannot be objectively measured, means that patients and physicians never have precisely the same definition of the problem to be solved, which complicates effective treatment. Often-cloaked causes make it hard to treat, too, as in the case of pain related to damaged nerves. As one anesthesiologist summed it up for me, "It is difficult to reliably influence what one does not understand."

However heterogeneous the individual experience of pain, its clinical management is highly standardized and pharmaceutical-centric in the Western health systems in which I have received care. During a long or tricky surgery, like the one to replant my hand, anesthesiologists typically administer a trio of drugs intended to keep the patient pain-free, perfectly still, and blissfully ignorant of all that transpires during the procedure. A painkiller, or analgesic, blocks the flow of nociceptor signals to the brain from tissue damaged by injury and surgery, thus limiting the information available for translation into unpleasant sensations and emotions. The analgesic also triggers release of chemicals that cause feelings of pleasure and well-being in a conscious person, causing that "no place I'd rather be" euphoria I enjoyed in the ER.

A drug in the edgy-sounding hypnotic category renders the patient unconscious, thus not only unaware of their context but also incapable of voluntary movement. By precluding the wakeful self-awareness that many neuroscientists believe is a prerequisite for pain and other mental states, like pleasure and fear, the hypnotic also reinforces the analgesic's effects. Finally, a paralytic drug reinforces the action of the hypnotic by relaxing the patient's muscles, thus preventing involuntary movements like gagging on a breathing tube. Outside the operating room, where patients generally need to be conscious and mobile, the acute pain management regimen can be simpler. Mine mainly comprised opioid analgesics— morphine in the hospital ER and recovery wards, and hydrocodone at home.

Researching pain, I noticed how mine had evolved over the course of my injury and recovery. I'd felt none until reaching the hospital—apparently a beneficiary of the brain's natural opioids, which can block pain-triggering sensory nerve signals en route to the brain in times of extreme stress, as described in chapter 2. When pain finally took hold of me in the emergency room, it felt unlike any I'd experienced: throbbing, searing heat and viselike pressure engulfing my entire hand—the hallmarks of inflammatory pain, plus some secret-sauce sensations my brain cooked up just for me. The analgesics dialed it down, but never enough to let me forget about it for long. This concerned Dr. Vargas, but he didn't deem it prudent to prescribe higher doses of the drugs. He had to balance the benefit of relieving my pain with the risks of blunting its protective qualities, and of addiction. And after all, I could bear it. So it persisted, intensifying between drug doses, after OT exercises, and other times for no apparent reason at all.

The pain aroused my worry and wonder in equal measure. My hand is supposed to be healing, I thought, so why does it hurt in exactly the same way as it did before surgery? What if the pain never stops, and I get addicted to the medication? How *alive* this poor thing is! What is going on in there, to cause this relentless, raging sensation? As designed, the pain also reminded me of my hand's fragility so that I would protect it. I did this with wearying gusto, monitoring my movements to spare it careless knocks and jolts, strictly adhering to my OT and drug regimen, and enlisting neighbors to perform essential but risky tasks—mainly opening new jars of peanut butter, food of the gods and staple of my one-handed-meal repertoire.

Just as inflammation spreads from injured to healthy tissue, that sense of fragility spread from body to spirit, causing me to question my capabilities and belonging—everything that normally makes me feel safe and hopeful. Such doubts didn't win much of my stretched mental bandwidth in daily life, but they pervaded my dream world. There, I embodied a Japanese man, and had just dug myself out of a suffocating avalanche, but my wife didn't believe me. There, I had prepared extensively for a violin recital, but my teacher and friends refused to attend, insisting I wasn't ready. There, I had never learned to skate, but was forced to compete in the Olympic ice dancing finals. The morning after such dreams, my most urgent self-care task was to shake off their poisonous messages: You are not yourself. You are not like anybody else. You are alone in this trial, and you may not be equal to it.

Looking back, I find these dreams achingly poignant, and more than a little comical in their hyperbole. But their counterpoints whipped up by my subconscious made me laugh out loud, even at the time: Sex dreams! Sex with cute guys I knew. Sex with cute women I knew. Sexy partners, outfits, and moves I could not imagine engaging with in real life. The dreams were racy and absurd. But in them, I was physically and emotionally whole, in sync with humanity, and *oh* so capable. Awaking from them, I felt a fleeting sense of my healthiest, pre-accident self.

Eventually, as my ravaged tissues healed, the chemical soup they'd stirred up dissipated, nociceptors in the area became starved of fuel, and the physical pain they triggered diminished. I needn't have worried about addiction to the hydrocodone; as the virtuous circle of healing accelerated, I simply began forgetting doses until I'd stopped taking it altogether.

The pain didn't completely disappear, though. It still burns and throbs today, and often comes with an aching stiffness and muscle fatigue. Fortunately, it never quite reaches its former intensity. And it has generally been more *off* than *on* since my hand healed—though ironically, it is more persistent now while my right hand spends most days gripping a pen, or tensed over my Mac keyboard, drafting pages for this book.

When the pain exceeds my patience for it, I run my right hand under cool water, or cradle it in the crook of my left elbow and encourage it to go limp, which seems to offer a little relief (though I couldn't say why; must research that). Sometimes instead of trying to chase the pain away, I let it hold my attention. I turn it over in my mind and tease apart its threads, curious about its expression du jour. I remember when the pain made me feel completely broken, yet breakable still, and just how much effort it took for me to distinguish between those feelings and my actual, improving prognosis. Now the pain reminds me of all that I have survived, and all that I have gained from my accident. It hurts, and I like it.

9

.....

At Home
with Strangeness

Two days later, on a bright Tuesday afternoon, Mom and I step through the front door of my one-bedroom prewar apartment in Brooklyn. I've been concerned this moment would prompt upsetting flashbacks of the accident, or a realization I could no longer live in what had been such a beloved home to me and my urban family—the site of big bashes, boozy girls' nights, chaotic kiddie brunches, the occasional intimate dinner date. Instead, I feel happy stepping into the large, sun-washed vestibule I use as a dining room.

Mom and I slowly walk through the few rooms, relieved to see that the professional biohazard cleaning crew hired by the building management has done a mostly, if not entirely, thorough job of washing away the blood I shed on the night of the accident. I notice a few missing articles—bedroom rug, clothing that had been strewn on chairs—that I later learn were bloodstained beyond salvage and discarded on Mom's instructions. Tired from the trip from Manhattan, I climb into my own bed for an afternoon nap, while Mom assesses the food stores in my kitchen. I appreciate her taking care of that, and that she doesn't mind my leaving her to it.

I fall quickly into the routine established at Erica's, awaking early each day, washing down a piece of toast with a cup of coffee, then launching into the first of three daily sets of hand exercises. Every movement results in some unnerving sensation, conjuring images of vibrating piano strings or snapping twigs, that convinces me I have screwed up the fragile landscape of my inner hand. I stick to the regimen, however, and record each completed repetition with a check on a notepad, taking heart in the rapidly accumulating marks.

After the morning exercises, I often take a half-hour walk through my neighborhood. Sometimes I go to the Brooklyn Promenade to sit on a bench and cry in the guaranteed privacy of a waterfront park in February. The crying fits feel like vomiting—involuntary, mindless, and often a relief. At midday, Mom prepares a simple lunch for us, like Campbell's tomato soup and a tuna salad sandwich, which is pure comfort food to me, then I do another round of exercises before sleeping for a couple of hours. In the late afternoon, I catch up on health insurance admin, speak with close friends on the phone, or poke around the internet for information about hands and spaghetti wrists. After dinner, I do a last set of exercises, wash my splint, write a barely legible, left-handed entry in my journal, then head to bed. The slow, monotonous days feel packed full.

Mom settles into her own routine, preparing our meals and

working her way through a long list of household chores she's created—defrosting the freezer, polishing silver, reorganizing the contents of my kitchen cabinets, repotting a crooked plant. I detest organizing, yet appreciate organization, and therefore her intent. But her frequent questions about where to find some cleaning supplies, or whether she can throw out this or that old item, rattle me. And it upsets me that tasks I am anxious about but incapable of doing—like finding a drugstore somewhere in Brooklyn that carries a special bandage I need to reduce scarring—keep falling to the bottom of her daily list. Knowing my accident has deeply disturbed her, too, I suspect she is seeking comfort in familiar activities. But there's no comfort in them for me.

As an avid lifelong musician, I will listen to anything at least once and have favorite artists across multiple genres. And I always have music playing in my home. But in these early weeks of recovery, it's as if the fears, problems, and fragile hopes dominating my thoughts are loudly audible, and I can only tolerate the sparest music on top of them. Gregorian chant and Bach's unaccompanied cello suites make up the soundtrack to our days, along with the modal choral works of Arvo Pärt, which make me think of a gray winter sky viewed through an icy, crystalline window: simple, beautiful, chilling, and a little sad. Music any more lush would overwhelm me and mock my mood. These selections reflect it in an oddly reassuring way, while somehow neutralizing its most painful aspects, helping keep anguish at bay.

I once read that for people who, like me, are passionate about music, listening to works we find compelling prompts the release of calming endorphins in the brain. That might explain why I, and innumerable other angst-ridden kids in the '80s, had kept the bleak music of Joy Division cranking throughout our bumpy transition into adulthood. But my own explanation for music's ability to console me is that the right piece at the right time vibrates in sync with my feelings, reminding me that whatever their nature, I am not alone in knowing them. They connect me to humanity and are therefore not to be regretted, though I sometimes wish them away.

My next appointment with Dr. Vargas comes just a few days after Mom and I return to Brooklyn, and during the trip into Manhattan I realize how much I've been looking forward to it. From deep within the turmoil of trauma and recovery, Bellevue has emerged an unlikely oasis, full of people who understand my ordeal and are gently coaxing me through it.

Dr. Vargas and I sit around the corner of a desk in an examination room, my bloated, discolored forearm upturned between us. Our heads bend toward each other, nearly touching. I refrain from asking questions, not wanting to distract him from the removal of my stitches. His suturing following surgery was meticulous; in a few years, the lines on my forehead will be more prominent than the scar on my wrist. Now his work is just as careful: He gently lifts each suture up with a pair of forceps in one hand, then snips it with scissors in the other. Eventually he breaks our silence.

"I showed your card around to everyone in the emergency room. They were really glad to hear you're doing well." I am touched that he has fulfilled my request and made a point of telling me so.

A bevy of junior residents shuffles into the room for a tutorial on spaghetti wrist, and as the residents pepper him with questions about it, I jump in with mine. He seems pleasantly surprised by my curiosity, and to enjoy satisfying it with the increasingly technical explanations I require. We are having fun. I ask how much of his training he's completed, learning he is in the final year of his second surgical residency, shortly to begin a prestigious fellowship. I suggest that, given how much he apparently enjoys professional studies, he consider subsequently pursuing an MBA. He throws his head back and laughs, mouth open so wide I can see his molars. "Yeah, then maybe I'll go to art school after that!"

Stepping out of Bellevue onto First Avenue afterward, I'm on a high. It's a gleaming, blue-skied day, I'm acquiring fascinating information about my injury, and Dr. Vargas's formidable facade is cracking. That matters to me, because I need to know that this stranger in charge of my case, in whom I've had to place so much trust, actually cares about me as an individual. And I can't know *that* if he doesn't return just a little of my warmth, reveal just a little of the person behind the title. Plus, I'm a nerd and want him to keep sharing his knowledge.

Early the following week, Mom accompanies me to my first full OT appointment. Given my perpetual exhaustion and mortal fear of tendon rupture, a round trip from Brooklyn to Bellevue on the subway—normally my much-preferred mode of transport—is unthinkable, requiring over a mile of walking, plus hiking up and down four long flights of stairs. So we've been hiring a neighborhood car service to make the trip. At 8:15 a.m., a battered butterscotch Lincoln pulls up in front of my building, and Mom hurries ahead into the frigid wind to open the curbside back door.

Hypnotic Middle Eastern pop wafts out of the car as I ease myself into the back seat, anxiously protecting my elevated arm despite its firm enclosure in the foam Guggenheim. Mom hovers just behind me with bent knees and open arms, a wool-wrapped coil waiting to spring should I misstep. Judging me settled, she reaches across my lap to fasten my seat belt. Though capable of performing the task myself (albeit slowly and clumsily), I let her do it, knowing I will have plenty of occasion to test my one-handed ingenuity over the weeks, and perhaps needing more justification for her company on this trip than the fact that I'm not quite ready to face all these Bellevue expeditions alone. I don't belong in my old world anymore but am still slightly wary of what I'll find in my new one.

"All set?" Mom asks, worried dark eyes contradicting her warm smile.

"I'm good, thanks," I respond as she rounds the back of the sedan to slide into her seat.

The car rolls forward and in minutes we are on the Brooklyn Bridge, where visions of my dead-of-night ambulance crossing two weeks prior compete with a sparkling view of Manhattan against a turquoise sky, flickering and expanding behind the steel suspension ropes whipping by.

At Bellevue, we move slowly from car to revolving doors, then down a ramp into the lobby—a modern, soaring glass atrium constructed around the 1930s brick edifice of the building. Bathed in natural light, the space teems with slow-moving patients and fast-walking, white-coated doctors, and absorbs all but the muted, indistinct remains of their conversations. From atop the ramp, this picture of industrious calm encourages me, though I know it belies the suffering and sorrow of people throughout the building. Level 1 trauma centers like Bellevue are the scene of a lot of sad stories.

Our driver's licenses, my red plastic patient identification, or "clinic card," and a doctor-signed appointment slip gain Mom and me passage through two police-manned checkpoints and a patient registration line, where I pay over $200 for my appointment thanks to a high-deductible insurance plan and a disagreement between Bellevue and my health insurance company as to whether outpatient therapy is an in- or out-of-network service. Finally, we arrive in the Upper Extremity Occupational Therapy Room.

Before my accident I, like many New Yorkers, associated Bellevue with its mean beginnings over two centuries ago as a public psychiatric hospital, and imagined it as a grim, squalor-filled building crammed with the forgotten mentally ill. But the facilities I've seen so far have been impeccably clean and seemingly well-equipped, if utterly lacking in the contemporary decor and comforts of the city's private hospitals.

The OT room's bright, almost cheerful aspect is another pleasant surprise. In the center of the room stand four white, kidney-shaped Formica-topped tables, each accommodating four patients and one therapist, and strewn with objects providing the day's rehabilitative challenges: lumps of putty in gradations of blue and gray, fuzzy piles of red and yellow yarn pom-poms, jars of green-swirled glass marbles, and small wooden pegboards with tiny metal pegs.

On the north and east walls of the room, two long banks of windows frame great, penetrating shafts of sunlight and a panoramic view up the East River. Two 1950s-era metal desks against the north wall support a couple of old computers and stacks of medical reference books, while waist-high shelves, packed tight with bins of colorful therapeutic tools and toys, line the east wall. On the river, stubby red and black tugboats chug back and forth performing the routine miracle of rotating an errant container ship on its axis, pointing it south toward New York Harbor's deeper waters.

On the south wall, immediately to the right of the door, a sternly efficient receptionist sporting a flaming-red beehive and pink plastic glasses sits at another vintage desk, checking patients' identification—yet again (do people *really* try to crash this party?). Behind her, scores of aging hospital policy memos paper a wall of moss-green cabinets.

On the west wall, just left of the door, a curtained bay encloses a single bed and chair where, I later learn, prisoners
undergo therapy, guarded by policemen and out of other patients' view. Next to the bay a red and blue Velcro dartboard
and two large, color-coded posters illustrating the human nervous and musculature systems hang over an industrial steel
sink, where patients wash city grime off their hands before
handling shared tools, and relearn household chores like dish
washing and food preparation.

In the far-left corner of the room, a waist-high counter sup-
ports a yard-long, covered metal vat of boiling water used to
soften the hard plastic sheets from which custom splints are
constructed. The splinting station, a shelved cart on wheels
parked next to the counter, houses gauze bandages, adhesive
Velcro strips, wire, measuring tools, and cutting implements.

Glancing first at the communal tables and brightly colored
toys, one might mistake the room for a kindergarten, if not for
its denizens. These include a man whose arm ends at the
elbow kneading a wad of gray putty with his stump; another
man, with an angry welt winding the length of his forearm,
laboring to pinch fluorescent clothespins from one pole and
attach them to another; and a woman with gnarled fingers
grimacing as she transfers a gallon of water from one bucket to
another by absorbing and disgorging it with a sponge.

The injuries across the room are a breathtaking collection
of misfortune—many the kind of shocking afflictions people
instinctively avert their eyes to avoid, before the mind can ask,
What if that were me? I might have shied away from them as

well, but having stared into the bloody mess of my own arm, I realize I can now not only look at terrible injuries without flinching, but I can also see the people behind them, and long to know their stories.

Deeply creased faces, calloused hands, and somber discount-store clothing—the anti-status symbols of the working poor—abound in the OT room because Bellevue treats people regardless of their ability to pay. Despite my corporate job, health insurance, and overpriced jeans, however, I already feel more at home in this room than I have anywhere else since the accident. I have a severe injury and all its accompanying pain, confusion, and anxiety about the future in common with my fellow patients, and this shared experience counts for much more than any differences between us.

Beth, the therapist who crafted my splint at last week's surgical checkup, greets Mom and me from across the room like a confident hostess welcoming new friends into her home for the first time. I'm suddenly embarrassed to have needed Mom here with me, but if Beth thinks it's strange I've brought her, she doesn't let on, graciously showing us both seats at a table near the door. She sits to my right at the end of the table, rests her elbows on it, then props her chin on her folded hands and smiles brightly, as if she's about to hear the titillating account of a girlfriend's recent date.

"Well, Miss Fogg, it's been a couple weeks, right? How are you doing?" she asks. I've noticed that all the therapists address us patients as Mr., Mrs., or Miss—a formality that feels antiquated, but in signaling respect perhaps helps build trust with a vulnerable population.

"Good, considering," I reply with a laugh. The absurdity of this whole situation never escapes me.

"Yeah, that was a *crazy* accident, right?" she responds, green eyes squinting sympathetically. Clearly the exploding toilet is noted in my file. "Well, let's see what we've got," Beth continues, unfolding a sterile cloth on the table in front of me and gesturing to me to remove my splint.

Laying my right hand palm up on the table, I use my left to release the Velcro straps that secure the close-fitting shell to my fingertips, palm, thumb, wrist, and forearm. Next, I gingerly pull on the tip of my right middle finger to free the hand from the splint, then lay it on the sterile cloth. I'm not yet used to the disturbing sensory incongruity of watching my left hand touch the denervated areas of my right hand while feeling nothing whatsoever in those areas. If I closed my eyes, I'd think I was touching another person. Yet I can still . . . almost? . . . recall the sensations of ruffling soft hair and smoothing silky fabric with my right hand, and wonder how quickly these sweet, tactile memories will fade. Dr. Vargas has prepared me for the fact that whatever sensibility I regain upon regeneration of the severed nerve will be highly impaired.

Finally, I tug off the fingerless jersey glove that protects my hand from chafing against the plastic, and again gently lay the hand down onto the sterile cloth. Even untethered, it retains the shape of the splint—a lobster claw, slightly agape—after two weeks of disuse and round-the-clock confinement. It doesn't feel, it doesn't move on its own, it still doesn't even look like a real hand. It may as well be a prosthesis.

"You don't have to be so careful," Beth chides. "It's *your* hand, and you're not going to hurt it just doing that." I'm not so sure about either of those statements. "Ah, you got your stitches out," she continues, leaning in to examine the wound. "The scar looks great! You won't believe how much it's going to fade. Dr. Vargas does an awesome job." Mom and I smile at each other. It's reassuring to hear a knowledgeable third party's endorsement of Dr. Vargas's work—though I've already started referring to him and his assisting residents as my "dream team" among family and friends.

Next, Beth uses a measuring tape, and instruments resembling a protractor and a single-fiber paintbrush, to measure the length of the scar, then the sensation, circumference, and range of motion of the wrist and fingers of both my hands. Ah, numbers! Finally, a way to understand my progress in this race toward recovery. Eager to know today's score, I crane to see the figures Beth records in her notebook, but realize I don't know whether they're good or bad.

"We can use your left hand as a benchmark for size and strength, and range of motion, because your right hand'll definitely get back to normal size and, we hope, close to full strength and range of motion," Beth explains. "But for sensibility, independent finger motion, and dexterity, the injured state has to be our baseline." She doesn't need to say that this is because recovery on these dimensions is highly variable, will surely be incomplete, and has a lot to do with luck. I get it: Never say *never*, never say *always*. No one knows where my finish line lies.

Finally, Beth asks how I typically use my hand at work and play, so that once the repaired tendons have healed, she can design an exercise regimen to help me develop the function needed for my routine activities.

"And I want to be able to play violin," I add, after covering essential activities like typing, cooking, and household chores.

"Did you play violin before?" she asks.

"Yes!" I reply. Dr. Vargas had asked the same thing. Do all medical professionals doubt the existence of musicians?

"Really? Oh, OK. Y'know, I had to ask because a lot of patients joke about that," Beth explains. "Like, they've lost a couple fingers and tell me they want to play piano, but they never did before." My first taste of amputee humor. Sick, and kind of funny.

After booking my next several appointments with Beth, Mom and I head out, my thoughts consumed by the therapeutic challenge ahead.

Back in OT by myself two days later, Beth seats me at a table with a couple of other patients, then leaves to fetch some supplies. Opposite me a young man sits in front of two stacks of large orange and yellow plastic cups—one short stack, one tall.

He inhales, grasps a cup on the tall stack with a trembling left hand, pulls it free, conveys it to the short stack, places it on top, exhales, then repeats the steps until all the cups stand in one stack. Red-faced and sweating, he pauses before performing the same exercise in reverse.

Lumpy, zigzagging scars cover the palm of his bloated hand, whose flesh is a deep, mottled pink. And long metal pins protrude from his fingertips, each pin topped by a small white plastic ball. The pins glint and undulate as he works, reminding me of sea urchin spines in a sunny ocean surge. As I watch him, I wonder what simple tasks I might, or might not, ultimately be able to perform.

"God, I hope I can do that someday," I sigh to myself.

The man looks up at me. "Oh, you will," he says.

Beth returns with a sterile cloth for the table, a bottle of hand lotion, and a manila file bearing my name. She pulls several typed pages out of the file that turn out to be Dr. Vargas's dictated report of my diagnosis and surgery. She reads aloud to reacquaint herself with the details of my case: "Complete transection of flexor digitorum superficialis, digits 2, 3, 4, and 5; flexor digitorum profundus, 2, 3 . . ." The words wash over me like those of foreign tourists on the subway, except I am dying to know what they mean.

No longer content merely to understand my injury in the simple terms Dr. Vargas has used to explain it to me, I'm determined to comprehend the minute details of the wounded anatomy, how the surgeons have repaired it, why they've done it that way. That operative report, the lucky find I didn't know existed, will be my Rosetta stone. I'm eager to dig into it, once I've obtained a copy from Bellevue's Department of Medical Records, since Beth can't release it to me.

She does, however, provide a tantalizing overview of its contents, referring to an anatomy book to show me exactly how many and which tendons, nerves, and arteries have been severed, and describing the functions they'd once performed. A visual learner through and through, I often see concepts as images in my mind, and draw charts and pictures to sort out my thoughts. Beth's illustrated tour begins to drive home the meaning of the medical terms I've heard so far, and the appalling extent of my injury. Studying manufacturing in business school, I learned that the more moving parts in a machine, the more likely it is to break, the more difficult to repair; so Beth's tour also explains why she and Dr. Vargas can't assure me of a good recovery. The surgeons having done their best, only my compliance with Beth's prescribed therapy can improve chances of that.

Recognizing this, and fortunate to have paid leave from work to focus on recovery, I've been very diligent with my exercises. "I can tell when people aren't keeping up with their routine because they're all stiff. You're doing *great*." I beam like a third grader entrusted with hall-monitor duty, clearly more enamored of the role of teacher's pet than I should be at my age, but willing to accept any reward for the hard work I have no choice but to do.

With ten minutes of the appointment remaining, Beth pushes her notes aside, dons purple surgical gloves, and squeezes some lotion onto my forearm, gently massaging it into the skin around the wound, then blending it downward from the wound to my elbow. "This will help reduce swelling by pushing fluids toward your lymph nodes," she explains, "and keep too much scar tissue from forming on the tendons, so they'll glide better." She adds this light massage to my daily regimen and wishes me a good weekend.

10

....

After the Unthinkable:
Psychological Recovery

On the morning of September 11, 2001, I had just stepped onto the thirty-seventh floor of my company's Manhattan headquarters when American Airlines Flight 11 plowed into the North Tower of the World Trade Center, less than one thousand feet away. The floor shuddered beneath my feet, and a long, metallic grinding sound rose above the babble of the waking office. I froze as my mind flipped through possible explanations like study flashcards: Not thunder; the sky is blue. Not from the building site next door; too loud and long. Instinctively turning toward the sound, I saw a thick curtain of indistinguishable stuff raining down outside the floor-to-ceiling windows of our north wall. I jogged over to investigate with a handful of colleagues.

Not far above us—just a forty-five-degree head-tilt up and right—black smoke and sporadic jets of flame erupted from a colossal maw ripped into the North Tower, edged with fangs of molten steel. We stood, dumbstruck, until a witness to the catastrophe told us what had happened. Eyes glued to the tower, I flipped open my cell phone and called my boyfriend, Marcus, an emergency room physician at a downtown hospital who was off work that day. "Hey. I'm OK, but a big plane just crashed into the World Trade Center. Some insane accident. You're going to be needed." He hardly needed a minute to grasp what I'd said; he encountered the incomprehensible every day. "On my way, call you later. Take care of yourself, OK?" he said, and hung up. It then occurred to me that the savaged building lacked floors and walls enough to contain all the dead and dying. Some were bound to fall, and it felt wrong to watch their last moments out of terrible curiosity. So I turned my back to the window, just as a colleague's yelp announced the first plummeting soul.

About fifteen minutes later, we were all online searching for news about the "accident" and calling loved ones to assure them of our safety when a plane crashed into the South Tower. A colleague who put two and two together before the rest of us yelled, "It's a *terrorist attack*—everybody out!" With the composure and determination of people used to overcoming challenges together, my colleagues kicked off heels, tossed off suit jackets, and hurried to the exits. I didn't move. The ground around our building looked like earthquake ruins. What if the attack wasn't over . . . or chunks of plane and building kept falling? Would we face more danger outside than inside? A colleague I didn't know stepped directly in front of me and, with pale blue eyes glaring into mine, said, "Get. Out. NOW." I snapped out of my looping threat assessment and joined thousands of building occupants thundering down the stairs. Seven minutes later I careened out of a ground-floor door onto a carpet of debris as the policewoman holding the door screamed, "GO! GO! GO! GO!" and pitched imaginary speed balls, urging us clear of the building.

The events of my slow trek home, to East Twenty-Seventh Street at the time, have solidified into a vivid capsule memory: A hulking rescue helicopter landing in the park next to our office building, defeated by impossible flying conditions around the towers. Human specks sailing down the towers' length, when I couldn't help stealing a backward glance. Thoughts of loved ones I couldn't reach due to an overloaded cellular network, and of people trapped in the towers realizing that help wasn't coming. People overflowing from neighborhood bars, drinking hard liquor and straining to hear the TV news blaring inside. A crowd of south-staring faces simultaneously contorting as one of the towers collapsed in a sickening roar, launching a tidal wave of rubble into the lower floors of our office building. And the stony feeling of my face through it all: furrowed brow, set jaw, stiff tongue against bottom front teeth. What I now know from experience is my mourning mask.

Then, five years later, I have to rescue myself when an explosion in my Brooklyn apartment blows my hand halfway off.

Born and raised in privileged circumstances, I naively once thought it extraordinary to have experienced two close encounters with death, let alone one. But exposure to traumatic events*—as victim, witness, emergency responder, or in a similarly intimate capacity—is utterly common. How common is "common"? The answer necessarily varies depending on how the question is asked, relative to what population, but the World Mental Health Survey Consortium offers one instructive benchmark. Surveying large samples of the general population on six continents, it found in 2015 that over 70 percent of all respondents reported exposure to one traumatic event, defined as threatened death, serious injury, or sexual violence. Over 30 percent reported exposure to four or more. Such statistics may shock, but cannot surprise, when one considers that the world supplies sufficient armed conflict, terrorist attacks, school shootings, natural disasters, interpersonal assaults, serious motor vehicle accidents, and other catastrophes to fuel a global twenty-four-hour news cycle.

I also thought it extraordinary to have ultimately emerged psychologically undamaged by these traumas. How, after all, could anyone feel safe and capable again, knowing that such things can happen and one is powerless to prevent them? How

----

* For purposes of this discussion, I use this term to mean "exposure to actual or threatened death, serious injury, or sexual violence," as it is defined in the American Psychiatric Association's *Diagnostic and Statistical Manual of Mental Disorders* (DSM), 5th edition. While this definition does not encompass all experiences that may be associated with psychological distress, I adhere to it because it describes mine, and helped me more efficiently identify relevant sources of information within the vast body of research on human response to adversity.

could anyone feel whole again, having been pierced to the core by the horror and grief of them . . . or bear to love or endeavor again, knowing that anything we cherish or build can be destroyed in an instant? But I did, and I am not at all unique in this respect, either.

Of course, it is true that, for all our astonishing, built-in survival capabilities, what doesn't kill us can shake the foundations of our lives and selves—what we believe, feel, do, hope for. In clinical terms, we may feel exhausted, confused, anxious, or depressed. We may avoid people and situations that remind us of the traumatic event. We may reexperience it through intrusive thoughts and images, and hyperarousal in the form of irritability, sleeplessness, difficulty concentrating, or elevated startle response. Trauma specialists believe some of these symptoms to be caused by the failure of our built-in threat-defense program, described in chapter 2, to deactivate as soon as danger has passed. At the extreme, we may develop post-traumatic stress disorder (PTSD), in which our clinical symptoms following a traumatic event persist and intensify, significantly impairing our ability to function at work, in school, in relationships, or in other important life domains.

And yet, a large majority of people exposed to a traumatic event don't develop PTSD. They suffer a few symptoms that resolve within several weeks or months, or even maintain psychological equilibrium and normal function throughout the experience and beyond. Manhattanites living south of 110th Street exemplified this after 9/11: A month after the attacks, 7.5

percent of surveyed residents reported symptoms consistent with a PTSD diagnosis, and 17.4 percent reported some symptoms of the disorder but below the diagnostic threshold. By six months, those figures had dropped to 0.6 percent and 4.7 percent, respectively.

What accounts for the variety in people's responses? Some Western cultural notions attribute it to volition and courage, implicitly making heroes of those who rebound from trauma, and failures of those who suffer long and deeply from it. But like our experiences of pain, or the conscious decisions we make to escape danger, our adaptability to trauma is a unique product of event characteristics and of interacting biological (including genetic), psychological, and environmental factors, many well beyond our knowledge, let alone our control.

For instance, the nature, severity, and duration of a traumatic event influence its psychological impact. So people exposed to traumas involving violence, like combat or assault, are much more likely to develop PTSD than those exposed to impersonal events, like accidents or natural disasters. Simply being biologically female can also elevate one's risk of developing the disorder, as can a history of trauma, or factors that may make emotional regulation and problem-solving more difficult, such as a serious mood disorder, low IQ, or lower level of education.

Conversely, people with higher levels of education tend to adapt better to trauma, as do those with financial resources and, especially, strong social networks that they can tap for practical and emotional support. Thus, the meta-tragedy in trauma: deeply entrenched social and racial inequities deprive innumerable people of such protective resources.

Research also suggests a number of inner resources that can promote healthy adaptation to traumatic events, as well as other acute stressors like the death of a loved one. An inclination to search for meaning, purpose, and opportunity in adversity is one; others include a realistic confidence in one's ability to influence circumstances, a problem-solving mindset, a religious or spiritual practice, and belief in the instructive value of both positive and negative life experiences.

This is by no means an exhaustive list of risks and protective factors influencing individual adaptability to trauma. And because we all experience trauma differently and bring a unique complement of resources into the task of coping with it, the means by which we do so can be counterintuitive, even disturbing, to the people in our lives. We won't rebound as quickly as some think appropriate, or grieve as long and strenuously as others think we ought. We'll "overshare" difficult emotions or maintain "too stiff" an upper lip. We might feel and express joy—even use humor, God forbid!—when others believe we shouldn't be capable of levity.

But there is no right or wrong way to feel about adversity, and there exist an infinite variety of paths through it—including positive emotion and humor, both of which have been associated with healthy adaptation. The moral of the story? It's pointless to compare, and unfair to judge, people's responses to trauma. We're all just doing the best we can with what we've got.

I dragged a few notable risk factors into my traumatic events—

two X chromosomes, a family history of serious mood disorders, and some personal history of depression and anxiety. However, I also benefited from a significant complement of protective factors, fundamentally including a strong family and social network; an advanced degree of education, mainly devoted to intellectual and practical problem-solving; and a level of professional and financial security that kept peripheral worries to a minimum and afforded me quality health care and time off for recovery. I leaned hard on these advantages, every single day, to navigate through the aftermath of my traumas, and particularly after my accident.

The tug-of-war between my risks and protective factors resulted in what I've concluded are my signature trauma-response symptoms: sleeping and weeping. For several weeks after 9/11, it was a Herculean effort to stay awake for more than a few hours at a stretch, and much of what I remember from that period is Marcus gently waking me to take calls or eat meals. I slept prodigiously after my accident, too—more hours than I spent awake, it seemed—certainly more than the side effects of painkillers, antibiotics, and an energy-sapping healing process alone could explain.

My weeping jags after the two traumas—always sudden, brief, and cathartic—differed only in their usual contexts: that solitary bench on the Brooklyn Promenade after my accident, and the 69th Regiment Armory near my Manhattan apartment after 9/11. Within days of the attacks, flyers covering every reachable exterior surface of the armory implored passersby to report sightings of missing loved ones last seen near the towers before the attacks. Their near-universal format: white printer paper, *HAVE YOU SEEN [NAME]* heading, a color photo of the missing beloved celebrating a happy life event, and a list of their identifying physical characteristics . . . scars, tattoos, birthmarks, gold-capped teeth. The colossal twin heaps burning downtown made it fantasy to believe that anyone would be found alive; their bodies would need identifying. I felt compelled to walk that path home, and to stop and read the flyers, and I was far from the only person wiping away tears as I did.

After my accident, I also had "reexperiencing" symptoms common among trauma survivors, with thoughts of 9/11 bombarding my consciousness, and prolific dreams about my feelings during recovery—fear, grief, and alienation gradually ceding to cautious optimism. I find it intriguing that my brain did not thrust gruesome accident replays on me while awake or asleep, especially given that the event resulted in devastating injury. Other people think it peculiar that I hardly worried about the real possibility of severe, permanent hand dysfunction. I am often tempted to satisfy my own and others' cravings for certainty by explaining these curiosities away but must continue to resist the inclination. Given the innumerable and unknowable factors that produced them, I'd be choosing, rather than revealing, the truth of the matter.

Psychological coping in the aftermath of trauma is not just about managing the clinical symptoms to which it gives rise.

It's also confronting our shaken foundations, the loss of those aspects of our lives and selves that used to sustain and guide us, but cannot in our new circumstances. It's a painful, confusing "dying while alive," in the words of a teacher of Tibetan Buddhism I recently encountered, who likens such transitions to the bardo between bodily death and rebirth in that tradition.

The existential keystone that wobbled for me after 9/11, and took a proper pummeling after my accident, was my mistaken belief that self-sufficiency was achievable and necessary. Since toddlerhood, when I first rebuffed my mother's help ("Becca do it BY SELF!"), I have craved the ability to explore, succeed, and fail on my own terms, and the strength to be the helper, not the helped. I also came to believe that I *had* to live this way. No complaints, no excuses, no second chances. I organized my young adult life accordingly, pursuing school admissions, degrees, and jobs like pieces of armor to fortify me on whatever quests I might fancy, and protect me from misfortune.

The strategy has yielded significant psychological and material benefits. But the beliefs underpinning it have caused me much unnecessary suffering and, at times, reduced my capacity to treat others the way I wanted to. I'd been challenging them in psychotherapy before the accident, slowly learning to accept our human vulnerability, and the accident accelerated that learning by dispelling my last delusions about self-sufficiency, beginning in my hallway when a fireman used his big, gloved hands to pry my left fingers off my bound wound so that he could relieve me in applying direct pressure to it.

I intuitively coped with the trauma by throwing myself into OT and studying the science behind my injury, which gave me a tenuous sense of control (to a hammer, everything looks like a nail, as the old saying goes). My dedication to OT yielded slow but steady improvement in strength, range of motion, and dexterity in my replanted hand. And just as my friend Scott had promised, learning about its anatomy helped me better recognize progress and tolerate disappointment in rehabilitation.

Very quickly, though, learning became a fascinating end in itself. With newfound appreciation for the severity of my injury, I wondered how I could have dodged fear until emergency services arrived, dodged pain until arriving at the hospital, and dodged PTSD altogether. Those questions sucked me into neuroscience, which, over the next fifteen-plus years, progressively led me to readings on human consciousness, psychology, genetics, and evolution.

I was also preoccupied by fuzzy, uncomfortable existential questions during recovery. *I just hope this all comes to mean something,* I wrote, almost weekly, in my journal of the first few months. I hit the books in search of answers to these questions, too, dipping into philosophy and religion, and consuming one "misery memoir" after another. Those stories of life-threatening and life-changing experiences—limb loss, cancer, addiction, brain injury, organ transplantation, severe mental illness, bereavement—offset my sense of alienation, and their endings hinted that someday, my wish to discover meaning in my trauma might come true.

For all these helpful coping mechanisms, I still needed my loose network of Samaritans—those loved ones, colleagues, neighbors, and strangers who implicitly and explicitly reassured me that I mattered to them, that I was not imagining my difficulties or my progress, and that life would improve. It was in what they said and how they listened, the meals they brought, the laundry done, doors held open without asking, tissues offered on a weepy subway ride, forgotten video-rental late fees waived, silly nicknames ("Hey, Lefty! Keep snoozing, I'll wake you up when we're boarding and escort you onto the plane first"), and so many other kindnesses.

They kept the virtuous circle of physical and emotional recovery turning, and me lightly tethered to their world until I could return to it. I did return, of course, when my hand had become sufficiently mobile, and my clinical symptoms of trauma response (all that sleeping and weeping) had subsided. But my experience of the trauma didn't end there.

One night in London not long ago, I was sitting in bed reading when a surge of grief and loneliness overtook me. The sudden change in emotional state perplexed me, since the book wasn't sad, nor was I brooding about any particular life issues at that juncture. It took a few seconds of mental exploration to realize it had been triggered by the song playing on the radio, which I had listened to a lot while recovering from the accident at home alone in Brooklyn, but not at all since. Called "Hang On Little Tomato," it came from an album of cheery lounge tunes a friend had given me, and its reassuring "things will look better in the morning" message had often prompted cathartic tears. All these years later, instead of bringing relief from the painful aftermath of trauma, the song reminded me of what it felt like to be in the thick of it.

The experience of trauma changes us. Like spilled ink, it seeps into every aspect of our being, perceptibly and imperceptibly tinting memory, perspective, identity, and beliefs, long after clinical symptoms fade. Prompted by almost any encounter with hardship these days, I recall the loneliness and anxiety provoked by needing help during recovery but not knowing where it would come from; the burden of having to spin optimism out of uncertainty for weeks on end; or the cramped-chest sensation accompanying upsetting emotions that need venting but defy articulation or lack a ready ear. It hurts to remember myself, and recognize others, confronting such difficulties.

I also recall what I have gained from coping with trauma. My occasional periods of anxiety and despair as a young woman left a residue that accumulated into a latent dread that some massive crisis could permanently lodge me in those excruciating states. But 9/11 and my accident served up irrefutable evidence that I was psychologically stronger than I had thought, and the dread began to awkwardly coexist with an unfamiliar faith. Not the naive kind that insists, contrary to all evidence, that everything always turns out OK, but the savvy kind that, as my friend Kathryne describes it, knows it's highly likely "you'll still be standing when something good finally happens again."

I've become much more comfortable asking for help. I'm better at recognizing others' emotional and practical needs in a crisis, and more skilled at addressing them because of the thoughtful support I've received myself. And strengthened by all these developments, I've taken personal and professional leaps to live in closer alignment with my values.

Someone is bound to label my personal evolution "post-traumatic growth" (PTG). Coined by trauma researchers in the 1990s, the term refers to positive psychological changes that some people report experiencing as a result of struggling through a severe crisis. However, I'm not convinced that it applies to me, as the authors' definition of growth requires a reshaping of beliefs that I did not experience, at least not to the degree implied. Rather, I attribute much of the positive change in my post-trauma life to a process of nurturing helpful perspectives, and starving harmful ones, that began long before 9/11 and my accident (and continues today). This assessment aligns with some trauma researchers' critique that instances of PTG are often simply a manifestation of an individual's pre-trauma traits and capabilities.

My primary concern with post-traumatic growth, though, is the tantalizing term itself. Belying the subtleties of the theory behind it, it implies that life's ups and downs can be distinguished and accounted for as neatly as debits and credits to a bank account. Interpreted through the lens of my national culture of origin—which detests unhappy endings and insists that anyone who works hard enough can achieve whatever they want—people could therefore misconstrue the theory as suggesting that traumatic experiences hold the possibility of unequivocally positive outcomes, and that those who don't experience them have only themselves to blame. That's an easy recipe for misery and callousness.

Whether inapplicable diagnosis, unsupported theory, or just bad branding, then, I reject the PTG label for my own development, much preferring a Brooklyn neighbor's take on how we change when we live through trauma. "Welcome to the Death Club," she said in a chance hallway conversation a few months after my accident and her father's death in hospice. "We've seen death up close, and we'll never look at anything the same way again."

The work of this figurative Death Club is to integrate death into life, before it inevitably consumes us. That means surrendering to paradox, learning to carry a belief in possibility alongside the visceral knowledge of profound and permanent loss, so that loss does not become the chief architect of our lives, causing us to shrink from what is enriching or necessary for fear of it. And it means learning to embrace the strange kind of happiness (there's no better English word for it, alas) that only travels with sorrow—like what my best friend, Jen, and I feel, knowing we can tell each other our scariest inner shit without scaring each other off; or what my siblings and I feel when we can address my father's frequent health emergencies with slick teamwork and gallows humor, despite our concern for him and the worries about our own futures that his situation prompts.

We members of the Death Club often recognize each other, sensing vulnerability that others do not, or noticing a particular ease with, and insight into, upsetting subjects that can only come from rigorous grappling with them. And we often seek out and support each other, knowing we share a familiarity with what is difficult to describe or bear, and a kinship that can reassure, without promising the perpetual safety we crave but know we cannot have.

In real life, that dynamic looks like this: In the summer of 2020, between pandemic lockdowns, I met up with members of my London running club for a trot around Hyde Park, and ended up doing the loop with a new one—a twenty-five-year-old guy who was stuck with me because he showed up too late to run with the fast boys and didn't know the route well enough to catch up with them.

"What do you do for work?" he'd asked.

"I'm writing a book," I replied, and within fifteen minutes, we'd offered each other the intimate stories of my accident and his father's recent, sudden death. We spent the next thirty minutes relating and witnessing the impact of our experiences, and parted with the warmth of good friends.

I can see the Death Club dynamic in my interactions with

Dr. Vargas, too. Examining my wound for the first time, he'd said, "Do you think you can look?" not, "I need you to look," subtly acknowledging the appalling nature of my condition, which I struggled to convey to other people in my life. And his enthusiastic support of my science studies suggested he understood that I needed to push my intellect to be sure that some recognizable part of "me" had survived.

There is freedom in this work of integrating death into life—freedom from the gnawing, depleting pain of resisting what we know to be true, and the squandered opportunity that results from not seeing the facts of our lives as they are. But it's beastly hard. Much harder, apparently, than I could admit to myself, until one morning on my way to work nearly a year after I'd recovered, when I tripped while galloping down the stairs of a footbridge over the West Side Highway. As my body flew out from under me, I felt that hot punch in the chest you get at the top of a big roller coaster drop, and only just managed to grab the handrail with both my hands and pull on it with all my strength, so that I could keep my skull from cracking on the step behind me. As my body stilled, I surprised myself by thinking, *Next time, I hope I just die.*

11
....

Music City TLC

Most everything that happens between my Bellevue visits is preparation for, or unwanted distraction from, my work there. I continue to follow my exercise regimen with a soldier's discipline and prepare questions for Beth and the surgeons in advance of appointments so I can efficiently milk them for information during our limited time together. I never arrive late for an appointment, and replay each one in great detail to family and the small number of friends who know about the accident, reinforcing what I've learned and making my progress feel more real by speaking of it to others.

Jen was the first friend I called about the accident, and she calls me every single day for weeks afterward. My best friend since college, she shoulders heavy emotional burdens in her family life and her work as a federal defense attorney, and faces them with courage, resourcefulness, and optimism. Still, she has time and empathy to spare for others, and day after day she listens patiently to whatever I need to talk about, and cheers the minute achievements that crown my struggles, like managing, with my left hand, to crimp the stiff-jointed fingers of my right hand another quarter of an inch toward its palm, or finding an illustration online that helps me understand how nerves work.

Most other friends and colleagues learn about my accident only as they call me about plans we'd made before it happened or when others tell them. It isn't that I don't want them to know; I just don't want to call them because it feels intensely awkward to broadcast the story, and talking on the phone saps my limited energy.

Testifying to the efficiency of the New York grapevine (or the power of an urban myth in the making), flowers, cards, and calls arrive steadily nonetheless. *Don't lose your spirit!* wrote one member of the work team I'd just joined, echoing the sentiments of many well-wishers. Apparently, my spirit, alternately called passion, joie de vivre, or forgiving attitude, is a big part of what people value in me. They don't want this trauma to "break" me, not only because they care for me but also, I suspect, because they need me to prove that trauma is survivable, that experiencing some terrible event themselves, they'd battle through it.

In quiet moments, I, too, fear the trauma might break me. So I keep the note from a better-known colleague on my bedside table, alongside the jumble of essential pill bottles: *You are a tough girl, you will get through it!* The vote of confidence means a lot coming from a woman who immigrated to the US alone at the age of twenty, speaking not a word of English, then went on to earn a master's degree and a job at a Fortune 100 company.

Neighbors I've never met slide notes under my door, offering all manner of help. To a few who say they've lost sleep worrying about me, I scrawl left-handed notes assuring them of my good spirits and improving health. My sister-in-law, Wendy, guides my young niece and nephew in making me a Valentine's Day care package filled with homemade cards (*hop you feal beter, aunty beca!*), chocolate, fancy lotions and soaps, and deliciously trashy magazines. Unpacking the beautifully wrapped contents, strewn with hand-cut, construction-paper hearts, I laugh with delight and wish yet again that my brother, Charles, and his family didn't live so far away.

Charles rarely calls himself, instead sending his good wishes through Wendy, and Erica doesn't visit. A former colleague-turned-friend, whose work I and others covered for months while she tended her child through a serious illness, never gets in touch.

Such radio silence hurts when I occasionally reflect on it, though I don't doubt these people care about me as much as I do them. I am just learning that there is no one way, or right way, to deal with trauma. Many people avoid those in troubling circumstances out of worry that they don't know the "right" thing to do or say. Others, overwhelmed by the sadness of a situation and/or pressing demands in their own lives, keep away in order to conserve their emotional fortitude for themselves. I realize I have done this myself, having semi-intentionally drifted from my parents during their divorce, and from a friend whose depressions I could not ease and which hit too close to home. I can hardly blame others for taking such self-protective measures now.

Some people are surprised that I don't ask, "Why me?" and attribute my can-do attitude to some kind of super-honorable stoicism. But I'm not stoic in the face of all hardship or disappointment. For one thing, I am perfectly capable of a good moan over the personal costs (imagined and real) of my cherished independence. Other people try to reassure me, and presumably themselves, that my accident must have happened for a reason. But I don't believe that.

I don't ask why the accident happened because I know the answer: Life is a crapshoot. I don't smoke, do drugs, sleep with strangers, ride motorcycles, jump out of planes, or neglect to buckle my seat belt, even in taxis—but my hand was still blown halfway off by an exploding toilet. With strength and prudence, we can ward off tragedy and trauma . . . until we can't. That knowledge doesn't depress me, it liberates me, finally disabusing me of a fallacy that has burdened me as long as I can remember: that if I work hard enough and make all the right moves, I can live a dreamy, sorrow-free life.

While I feel certain my accident didn't happen for a reason, I fervently hope it will come to mean something; that if I have to be physically and emotionally scarred, I will also be changed for the better in some unforeseeable way. I can't stomach the possibility of fighting through the ordeal just to return to life exactly as it was. I work obsessively at OT, then, believing the effort to be both meaningful in itself and the only possible route to the longed-for, larger meaning.

The satisfaction of coaxing my right-hand joints to limber up, or improving my left-handed penmanship, also motivates me, as does my newfound fascination with medical science, and the respect and encouragement of my medical team and many well-wishers. It's easier to run, and harder to quit, a race when a big crowd has shown up to cheer you on. Easier, but not easy.

By the third week after the accident, I routinely find myself lying in bed at night, hand burning like a tiki torch, waiting for the most recent dose of hydrocodone to kick in. I've begun to think of my hand as a crying newborn and plead aloud with it in the dark like a madwoman. "Shhhhh. Oh, baby, you're killin' me," I chide affectionately. "Please, you have *got* to quiet down!" Now that I know the burning sensation characterizes healing tissue, I can't be too angry at my hand for keeping me awake. Unfortunately, however, the price of insomnia is greater than mere fatigue, as anxious thoughts take advantage of the absence of daytime's distractions to camp out in my mind and taunt my hopefulness.

Mostly I brood about work. Given my rate of recovery, there's no chance I'll have the stamina, concentration, or hand functionality needed to do my job by the date I've committed to returning to work. My concern about telling my boss (who has been nothing but supportive) that I need more time off mingles with the insidious notion that my mind might be as broken as my body, and I will return to work to discover I no longer excel at it. I also worry that work-induced stress and fatigue will compromise my physical recovery.

Finally, this tangle of anxieties snowballs into existential distress as I realize I don't even care about work anymore and can't imagine ever caring again. I have many interests and don't define myself entirely by my job. But professional challenge and accomplishment have always been important to me. How could that have changed, and so suddenly? Who will I be after all this is over? What will I *do*? Eventually, mercifully, I fall asleep.

In daylight hours a more practical question rears its ugly head: that of how I will care for myself once Mom leaves the following week to nurse her husband, Charlie, after his urgent hip surgery. I've figured out how to perform many self-care tasks myself, like dressing and bathing, but each one requires an inordinate amount of time, patience, energy, and even strategy. For instance, one-handed execution of the formerly simple process of opening a pill bottle, shaking a couple of pills out, and swallowing them with water now requires twenty-seven individual movements (of course I counted), starting with my sitting on the floor and wedging the bottle between the rubber soles of my sneakers so I can concurrently push and turn the childproof cap with my left hand. Multiplied by six medications taken throughout the day, the task would claim a material portion of my waking hours if I didn't apportion the day's doses in advance, leaving piebald piles of drugs on my bedside table that I send skittering to the floor while groping for my water glass at night with my unpracticed left hand. The thought of trying to manage grocery shopping, meal preparation, and house cleaning on top of such mission-critical activities utterly deflates me.

It also upsets me that Charlie has the greater claim on my mother's assistance despite my equal need—or perhaps greater need, as I see it, considering the traumatic nature of my accident—and the fact that his grown children live minutes away from him. In clearheaded moments I understand that his children have children and jobs of their own to manage, also that Charlie will do best with Mom's consistent and reassuring care. But mostly, I struggle to accept the lonely reality that I bear sole responsibility for my recovery. I feel like Tarzan swinging through the jungle: strong arms and plenty of vines to ride, but not a single one to carry me the whole distance. And each moment of transition—when I have to drop one vine, hang in the air unsupported, and lunge for the next— frightens me. Erica was the first vine, Mom the second; I need to find the third.

I bounce my ideas off Mom—hire a housekeeper or home health aide, ask the church down the street if they can send visitors—but her anxiety about the situation gets the better of her, and she finds imperfections in each option. I know a solution hides somewhere along the lines considered, but I lack the energy to convince her of this, or to research the options without her help. I suggest instead that I should return with her to Nashville, just long enough to catch up on my sleep and figure out a home care plan. Mom's expression turns instantly from dour to delighted. "That's a great idea! That'll work. Charlie will be so happy we're coming home. I'll call the airline. I bet we can get you back on frequent flier miles." And just like that, she's a parent again, taking charge of what I cannot.

The next day I call Dr. Vargas for permission to execute the plan. Guarded by vigilant gatekeepers, Bellevue physicians can only be reached through their academic offices, so I call the NYU Institute of Reconstructive Plastic Surgery to leave him a message. He always returns my calls (which I am careful to specify as nonemergencies) within a day, but often during my frequent naps. "You're not an easy person to reach," he said during one game of voicemail tag. Somewhere in the recesses of my cotton-filled brain, I resented that comment.

This time, I'm awake when he returns my call. I explain the unsustainable situation in Brooklyn and ask his opinion of the plan to go to Nashville. My esteem for him and his commitment has grown as I've seen more of the human tragedy that surrounds him at Bellevue, and I dislike revealing my vulnerability by asking if I can "run home to Mommy." But his response reflects no disrespect, only his characteristic clinical rigor.

"Yes, you can do that," he says, "if you find a board-certified hand surgeon there who will read your file before you go and agree to see you immediately if you have a tendon rupture or any other complications. And I don't want you away from Bellevue for longer than two weeks."

"Great, thanks—we'll find someone at Vanderbilt," I say, relieved to have bought a couple more weeks with family to figure out my subsequent self-care plan.

"You should be aware, though, that my team and I will be rotating off your case at the end of the month," Dr. Vargas continues. "The next chief will be fully apprised of your situation, and you'll receive excellent care. But if you stay in Nashville a whole two weeks, you won't see us again."

"Oh . . ." My heart sinks. Just when I think I've worked it all out, everything falls apart. What will I give up? I need it all: rest, the comforts of home, Mom's care, and the team of surgeons I trust—the only people who have been with me since the beginning, who truly understand what I'm going through. "Um . . . OK, that's good to know," I say, trying to disguise my worry, trailing off as I weigh the decision. Snapping to, I thank Dr. Vargas and hang up the phone, having just decided.

Visits to Nashville while my parents were together used to knock me down. Their unhappy marriage and depressions made our family life a minefield of anger, resentment, and despair, confusingly punctuated by moments of genuine harmony and wrenching détente that I learned early to distrust.

Now that my parents are both happily married to other people, however, Nashville offers respite.

Built in the 1920s, Mom and Charlie's home is a soothing cocoon of big-windowed, high-ceilinged rooms designed to be cool in the Southern heat; soft carpets and elegant but comfortable furniture; and everywhere the eye rests, colorful objects and artwork collected by Mom and Charlie on their travels, which sing together without melting into homogeneity.

Whenever I visit, I feel as though I'm staying in a little boutique hotel, and only the distant sounds of a baseball game wafting up from the kitchen TV—calming white noise I remember from childhood—dispel this pleasing illusion. Combined with the warmth with which Mom, Charlie, and Charlie's family always receive me, their home makes Nashville an oasis to which I willingly retreat once a year . . . though I usually bolt after a few days, pining for New York City's manic pace, and keen to avoid regressing into adolescent irritability.

My visit following the accident is good for both me and Mom. With pleasure and cheer, she makes sure Charlie and I eat well, sleep comfortably, and have plenty of upbeat books and DVDs for non-taxing entertainment. Charlie and I compare battle scars and therapy regimens, and the three of us often enjoy just sitting and talking together at the end of a day.

Though I feel no less a solitary stranger in my new, post-accident life than I had in the days just after the event, ensconced in familiar comforts with Mom and Charlie I feel less disoriented. Mercifully, I begin to sleep six to eight hours at a stretch, thanks to my psychiatrist Dr. Berg, who prescribed a mild sleep medication and an over-the-counter antihistamine to keep me knocked out for a few early-morning hours after my pain medication predictably wears off. Dr. Vargas had deemed it unwise to prescribe any more or stronger pain medication, and was impressed by Dr. Berg's solution to my pain-induced sleeplessness. Dr. Berg was impressed that my surgeon respected the contribution of a shrink.

I have lots of space to myself at Mom's, which I appreciate after weeks of sharing small New York apartments; and I have plenty of time, too, since I am skipping several hospital visits. So in addition to faithful continuation of my daily two-hour OT regimen, I begin squandering a bit of my increasing energy on pleasurable activities like reading escapist novels (Dorothy Sayers's Lord Peter Wimsey mysteries, European travelogues), and surfing the internet for new rugs and bedding to replace those that had been discarded due to accident mayhem.

Having found the iconic *Gray's Anatomy* medical text online, I also study hand anatomy and function. I make color prints of the relevant pages, then pore over the tangle of red and black lines and letters in search of the words Beth and Dr. Vargas use—*flexor tendon, median nerve, musculotendinous juncture*—painstakingly jotting down questions with my left hand to ask when I return to New York.

My voracious appetite for this knowledge surprises me because I've never been particularly drawn to the sciences, and the learning both calms and thrills me. Like an explorer with her frontier map, I keep the illustrations within arm's reach and consult them regularly. They show my destination—the functionality my surgical repair and OT have been designed to recapture to the fullest extent possible—and will enable me to appreciate my progress toward it.

On a couple of occasions I venture out with Mom and Charlie for an early dinner at a nearby restaurant. The overly rich Southern fare does nothing to stimulate my appetite, but the taste of a social life hits the spot, and for the first time since the accident I can envision wanting to be among people again, if not anytime soon.

Gadi, a dear friend from business school, offers another opportunity to step out when he drives the five-hour round trip from his home in Huntsville, Alabama—after working a full day and flying on business thirty times in the prior thirty days—just to take me to dinner one night. When he calls to tell me of his intent to visit, including the fact that he'll have to return home the same night to make a meeting the next morning, I protest that so short a trip will be too tiring for him. He shouldn't come, I'll see him the next time he's in New York. "If all I have time to do is give you a hug and leave," he responds, "then that's what I'll do. I won't believe you're OK until I see you myself."

He arrives at the front door with a chocolate cake bearing the frosted inscription *Get Well, Becca*, gives me the promised hug, and takes me out for a burger (of which I manage to eat half—record consumption, given my antibiotic-suppressed appetite) before heading home in an explosive thunderstorm. Standing at Mom's front door as he pulls his rented maroon Ford Escort out of the driveway, I watch until his blue-blinking Bluetooth earpiece disappears behind a curtain of rain.

Several days after arriving in Nashville I notice that Maggie, my best friend from high school, has left a message on my cell phone. On paper, Maggie and I have little in common. A devout Christian from an old Nashville family, she was presented at a society debutante ball during college, participates in a 5:00 a.m. weekly Bible-study group, and has been raising a young daughter by herself since her marriage ended.

I am . . . none of those things: spiritual but not religious (as the online dating sites prompt people like me to describe ourselves), an ever-single, child-free Yankee who'd never quite felt at home in Nashville and hightailed it back north right after high school.

But what Maggie and I have in common—curiosity about everything, a love of human diversity, pleasure in goodwill given or received, and a keen sense of responsibility for the quality of our own and others' lives—is much more fundamental to the way we live than our differences, and has always transcended them. I'd called Maggie my first day in town, craving her uniquely optimistic yet pragmatic brand of encouragement, and am delighted to hear her return message.

"HeEYYyyyyy!" she drawls in her signature greeting, which I've marveled at for close to thirty years. Like a fire-engine siren, it starts somewhere in the middle of her vocal range, abruptly scoops upward, then floats slowly down to the bottom, fading out completely just before she gathers her breath to do it all over again: "How're YEWwwwww?! I tried to reach you earlier to see if it was OK with your mom if I stopped by around six," she rattles on in the message, "but you didn't pick up. So, Ceci 'n' I are coming over because it's the only window I have to see you, and your mom will just have to deal!"

When we kids were growing up, Mom didn't like our family time, or perhaps whatever fragile peace we might have been enjoying, to be interrupted unexpectedly. So I had usually asked permission to invite Maggie over, though she lived just around the corner. These days, I don't think Mom will mind a good-natured surprise visitor. Living in a home without volatility, she no longer needs to be the anxious nurturer of stability. And she has always been fond of Maggie, too. I call Maggie back to say her timing is perfect.

Thirty minutes later she shows up at the front door, tall, slim, and unnaturally but attractively platinum blond, grasping her six-year-old's hand with one hand, clutching a video cassette and Bible to her ample breast with the other. Flashing her dazzling Princess Diana smile, which earned her all kinds of attention in the 1980s, she momentarily drops her daughter's hand to tap at the glass window in the front door. Prominent crow's-feet flare out from her large blue eyes like a ballerina's trompe l'oeil eyelashes. She's always had them—the result of fair skin and frequent smiling, rather than age.

"I'm so glad this worked out," she trills. Leaning down to her daughter, she says quietly, "Ceci, can you say hello to Miss Becca?"

Ceci, who hasn't seen me in a couple of years, huddles to her mom's leg and whispers the prompted greeting. Sensing her mother's excitement, though, she smiles broadly in anticipation of some unknown pleasure to be revealed during their visit, and unabashedly scans the room behind me for clues as to its nature.

I squat down to greet her eye to eye. "Hey, Ceci—thanks for coming over! Would you like to go upstairs and see my old dollhouse?" She nods vigorously, and Maggie winks conspiratorially at me. We've just won at least fifteen minutes of uninterrupted talk time.

In the refinished attic that serves as a playroom for Charlie's grandchildren, Maggie and I show Ceci the dollhouse, turn on a kiddie TV channel, then settle ourselves on the couch in front of the TV. Turning to face me, Maggie speaks in a low, urgent tone.

"Thank *God* you're OK. I was so worried about you, and I can't *tell* you how relieved I am to see you doing well. I mean," she qualifies, appraising my splint and thin, wan face, "looks like you've been through all heck, but I can see you're pulling through. Talk to me now . . . what *happened*?"

She listens, eyes crinkled in sympathy, as I recount the

story. Inwardly, I wonder why I never tire of telling it, and in such great detail. Because I want the people I care most about to understand my experience? Yes, but telling the story can't accomplish that, because even *I* don't understand it—what exactly happened, what had caused it to happen, what its impact has been and will be. Sometimes it doesn't even seem possible that it could have happened.

Maybe those are all the reasons why I want to tell the story over and over again: it's the catechism I recite to explore and fix in memory the facts of the accident, to proclaim its veracity, and to justify to myself and others the magnitude, if not the precise nature, of its impact. Yet even my most detailed account of events conveys little of my experience that night. I come closer to the truth in telling Maggie I've never felt an emotion as powerful and consuming as the terror that coursed through me as I awaited the ambulance.

Maggie is holding my left hand by this point. "I am *so* sorry. I've been praying for you, and just thank Jesus you're so strong, and that you have lots of people to help you." Though I don't share Maggie's unwavering faith, I have always liked having it on my side.

Ceci has grown tired of the dollhouse, so we steer her to a vintage Barbie doll and shoebox packed with bubblegum-pink, acid-green, and smiley-face yellow Barbie clothes. When she gets bored again in another fifteen minutes, we'll pop in the videotape of Maggie dancing and winning last year's Hotlanta Dance Challenge in the American Smooth category.

On weekends in high school, while the cheerleaders, athletes, and student council representatives drank and flirted at parties, Maggie and I enjoyed tame nights in at one of our homes, making chocolate chip cookies and watching videos of old musicals or of our respective performances in school plays and dance recitals. But for the happy addition of Ceci, tonight feels like old times.

Back on the couch again, Maggie tells me of her own accident and rehabilitative challenge—a shattered wrist sustained in a fall while dancing two years ago. The bones had thrust through the skin, her companions had panicked, and so despite excruciating pain, she'd had to organize her own transfer to the hospital. Worse, despite intense pain and confinement to a cast, she'd had to show up to work the very next day, having expended her limited sick days nursing Ceci through a few recalcitrant bugs.

Maggie's story upsets me on many levels. She'd had no time off work for recovery. She'd had no one at home to help her through the crisis, whereas I've had constant family support for several weeks. And I, absorbed with my big-city life, hadn't even known she'd been hurt. But her tone is devoid of self-pity; she tells her story only to encourage me.

"I have to show you this," Maggie says, opening her Bible to a bookmarked page and laying her long, well-manicured fingers down on it. "The first day I had to dress Ceci for school with my wrist in a cast, I was beside myself. Everything I pulled out of the drawer had all these buttons and bows," she says, throwing her hands up, laughing. I laugh, too, able to appreciate how absurdly ambitious the most mundane task becomes when attempted one-handed. "I was so frustrated and scared, thinking how the *heck* am I gonna take care of us for a whole six weeks like this?! And I'm trying not to cry in front of her, but of course she keeps saying, 'What's the matter, Mama?'" Maggie shakes her head recollecting this episode, much like those that make up my every day.

"I'm sorry," I say, empathizing too little, too late. "I didn't know about all that. I wish I'd been checking in with you more, and that you'd had help."

"Oh, that's OK! Honestly, you couldn't have done anything. I'm only telling you all this because I did get through it, and I want you to know that you will, too." She turns the Bible on her lap to face me. "Anyway, somehow I get Ceci dressed and out the door, and I say, 'Lord, I can't do this alone, you're going to have to help me.' And I pick up my Bible, open it up to a random page, and see this." She points to Psalm 51:8: *Let me hear joy and gladness; let the bones you have crushed rejoice.* "Isn't that amazing?!"

"That *is* cool," I concur. Despite my agnosticism, I'm always willing to appreciate coincidences that augur well for me and my loved ones.

"Whenever I got overwhelmed after that, I just read that verse and remembered that God was with me and I had everything I needed to get through that awful time. And you do, too, Becca. Think of all the hard things you've done and been through in your life, and you've always landed on your feet. You aren't alone, and you'll do it."

Though Mom and Charlie cheer me on daily, I relish Maggie's pep talk. I hoard everyone's encouraging words, to replay them in moments when my rehabilitative fervor needs stirring. Rereading the Bible verse, I contemplate writing it down, then decide not to. Maggie's words inspire me more.

"But," she continues, "you're going to have to work hard. It's easy to blow off the therapy, but you can't, because there's just a short window where you can improve, and once it closes, you're stuck wherever you stopped. See this?" She presses her thumb and fingertips down on the coffee table in front of us, her palm cupped as though trapping an insect. "I can't flatten my hand out completely. That's because I only gave therapy a B-plus effort. I thought that was pretty darn good, considering I was holding down a job, taking care of Ceci, and all that. Now I wish I'd given it an A-plus effort, because I could have, and it's a real pain not being able to flatten it out. Trust me, you don't know all the things you need to be able to do until you can't do 'em. So, *you work your butt off!*"

I take Maggie's warning to heart, because the OT is already feeling burdensome, and it's only going to get more intense once my tendons have healed. And if she, always a straight-A student who gave every endeavor maximum effort, had been tempted to slack off on therapy, I will surely be more so. But I don't want to suffer the regret she does. I vow again to take full advantage of my small window for improvement, and thank Maggie for a lesson only she could teach me.

Finally, we watch the video of her winning dance performance. Though Maggie and I haven't seen each other regularly in years, my first thought seeing her perform is *How did she get so good without my knowing?* Light and fluid, her steps seem perpetually to anticipate, but never arrive at, a resting place; and the evident but G-rated chemistry between her and her partner is so engaging as to make all the competitive couples disappear. Her gown, at first glance just another shimmering chiffon number, is cut much more modestly than her competitors', though every bit as flattering and sexy. As always, I admire how confidently and nonjudgmentally Maggie integrates her deep faith into a thoroughly modern life.

Ceci's bedtime looms, so we herd her downstairs, where she dares to blow me a goodbye kiss. Maggie and I hug tightly, knowing it may be years before we speak again, but that when we do, we'll pick up right where we left off.

Each day in Nashville, favorite people from all corners of my life call to check on me. Still fighting fatigue and sensory overload, I keep my cell phone off and return at most two calls a day, though each one compensates for the energy it consumes by yielding critical encouragement and advice. Dad calls most days, his consistency a great feat of focus given he lives with bipolar disease, and therefore all the more appreciated. He remembers and asks about my progress toward various therapeutic goals, commends me on my hard work at recovery, then gently cautions me against trying to do too much, too soon—a mistake he knows I often make.

To Linda, a former boss, I confide my fever pitch of anxiety about returning to my new job at the company where we've both worked for a number of years. She assures me there is no need to rush back ("The work will wait, and in six months no one will even remember you were gone") and reminds me to rely on my "core"—the colleagues with whom I've become close over the years—for support while I readjust to the work world and settle into my new role.

A couple of friends suggest I structure my reentry as they did theirs following maternity leave, working part-time for two weeks, then gradually adding days until a full week feels manageable. A Brooklyn neighbor recommends someone who can clean my apartment every two weeks, beginning as soon as I return to it. Each conversation strikes a few more lines off my list of worries and leaves me flush with gratitude.

In the end, Dr. Berg and Jen solve the dilemma of how I will care for myself at home alone. Dr. Berg suggests I ask my friends to take turns visiting me, so that every few evenings (my chosen interval, as more frequent visits would exhaust me) I can look forward to some company, as well as help cooking, tidying, grocery shopping, and other chores that try my physical and mental capacity.

Jen offers to put together the visiting schedule, and I give her contact information for around twenty friends and acquaintances I think may be willing to help. She emails them immediately, and cheerfully reports back a few days later that the response has been so strong she can't accommodate everyone. The scruples I'd expressed about inconveniencing our enlistees vanishes with this news; Jen has been right again.

"Would you hesitate to help any of these people if they needed you? Of course you wouldn't," she had said, answering her own question before I could. "Then how could you possibly think they wouldn't want to help you?" She gives herself and her family—husband Cody, gorgeous little boy Jake—the first slot. "Cody wants to make you a cassoulet for dinner. Is it OK if we stay the whole day so he can make it there?"

The morning I leave Nashville for New York—the day before my last appointment with Dr. Vargas and his team—I am well rested and prepared with plans to cope with my most immediate challenges. In recent nights, dreams of unforeseen opportunities and rewarded leaps of faith have replaced nightmares of asphyxiation, rebuffed tenderness, and lost or doubted talents. I board the plane ready, excited.

I arrive at my apartment close to midnight. In my absence, the heavy, sixteen-foot-long replacement rug and several boxes of new bed linens I'd ordered have been delivered and stacked high in front of my door. I am barricaded out of my home. All my confidence and determination, tenuously maintained during the grueling seven-hour journey home, instantly dissolve. I clap my left hand to my mouth to muffle a wail of despair; tears stream over my hand while I try to focus my mind on a solution. I can't move the packages, can't wake the neighbors begging for help *again*, can't face the people who'd last seen me in a blood-soaked negligee, can't stay in the hall all night.

What am I going to do . . . what am I going to do . . . *what am I going to do?*

Finally, judging another midnight drama with the neighbors the greatest evil, I set to the ill-advised task of shoving the rug and boxes aside with my shoulders and hips, lifting some of the lighter boxes between my elbows. The exertion-induced rush of blood into my splinted forearm feels dangerous, but I don't stop. I clear the door and, after dropping the keys several times in attempting to unlock it with my unpracticed left hand, heave myself inside. Leaving everything outside, I close the door behind me, then sob nonstop while I put myself to bed.

12

Pins and Needles: Peripheral Nerve Regeneration

Surgeons who want to impress upon their trainees the psycho-social importance of hands might cite the harrowing experience of New Zealander Clint Hallam. In 1998, an international team of surgeons grafted the right hand of a deceased Frenchman onto Hallam's forearm, some years after he'd lost his own in a circular-saw accident. Enabled by a number of late-twentieth-century medical innovations, the complex procedure yielded impressive results. Within a year, Hallam had gained enough motor and sensory function in the donor hand to perform many activities of daily living with it, and his case was widely lauded as the world's first successful hand transplant.

In 2001, one of the surgeons agreed to amputate the donor hand, citing irreversible physical rejection as justification. However, interviews with Hallam suggested that this was not his only reason for pursuing the procedure. The donor hand was noticeably bigger, lighter-skinned, and less hairy than his surviving hand, and bore scars, grafts, and excess flesh from the transplant procedure. The mismatch made him uncomfortable, and shocked others so much that he often hid the donor hand with clothing and gloves. After two years of struggling with his altered body image, an onerous immunosuppressant drug regimen, and numerous bouts of physical rejection, he'd become disgusted with and "mentally detached" from the donor hand and could no longer bear to be physically attached to it.

If aesthetics and social acceptance strike you as trivial concerns in Hallam's circumstances, consider all that we rely on hands for beyond physical agency. Superficially, they're an always-on channel for broadcasting affiliation, status, and values, as women Olympians do with their patriotic nail art; British aristocrats with family coat-of-arms rings; American high school grads with class rings; Hindu brides with henna tattoos; and Catholic nuns who wear wedding bands after betrothing themselves to God. The more I consider such symbols, the more of them I notice, and it's interesting to consider why we want other people to know what we tell them with hand decoration.

Hands bear the marks of our professions, hobbies, and habits. A coder keeps her fingernails short to facilitate typing. A classical guitarist keeps their right fingernails long for plucking and strumming. A builder may develop calloused palms from laboring with tools, and a massage therapist may maintain soft ones by working scented oils into clients' skin. Nicotine-stained fingertips suggest a heavy smoker; ragged nailbeds suggest a nervous nibbler; and pinpricked thumbs an avid needleworker.

Hands in motion signal our feelings with terrific economy, as with the internationally recognized thumbs-up for "good," or the Italian *cornuto* (index and pinky raised, palm out) for "fuck off!" They extend greetings and blessings, such as the Muslim *adaab* (slight bow with fingertips raised to one's forehead, palm inward), the Filipino *pagmamano* (forehead bent to an elder's outstretched hand), or Spock's Vulcan salute on *Star Trek* (palm out, double-fingered V with outstretched thumb). They refer with a finger-point, mimic to express desires (check, please!), play clapping games and make shadow puppets, create works of art and, by writing and typing, transmit information and ideas among people and over time.

Hands also amplify the spoken word, as poet Amanda Gorman's did so exquisitely with her recitation at the 2020 US presidential inauguration and they can obviate the need for it entirely, while conveying meaning in ways that speech alone cannot. People conversing in American Sign Language, for instance, can express multiple ideas simultaneously, and entire sentences with a single gesture. And classical Indian dancers tell ancient legends through a standard repertoire of gestures called *mudras*—which, according to a medieval Sanskrit text, crucially enhances the narrative: "For wherever the hand moves, there the glances follow; where the glances go, the mind follows; where the mind goes, the mood follows; where the mood goes, there is the flavor."

Symbolically, hands infuse spoken language with flavor, too. I've been equally irritated and amused by the frequency with which I've had to strike *grasp, on the one/other hand*, and similar imagery from this manuscript, not wanting to distract you with unintended puns. I couldn't possibly deny myself all of it, though. It's too useful, too plentiful. Why? One contemporary philosopher suggests that humankind's hand-intense interaction with the physical world naturally inclines us to consider it in manual terms (though not exclusively). For instance, I use the same coffee mug every day not just because it holds a lot of coffee, but also because its handle is easy to hold with my impaired right hand. It's hardly a leap from there to apply manual terms to our conceptual world. We grasp objects, and ideas are the objects of our mind. Why not grasp ideas, too?

And then there is touch. Delicate, exposed, and sensitive, our hands ask for care and offer it with touch, like a teammate's congratulatory backslap, a friend's consoling hug, or a lover's arousing caress. When it is welcome, interpersonal touch is pleasing in itself. It enhances well-being in many more ways besides, strengthening social bonds; promoting trust, cooperation, and generosity; and acting on the nervous system to alleviate stress, feelings of social exclusion, and physical pain. And we suffer when deprived of it.

While we intuitively understand hands' multidimensional influence on our lives, it is also supported by a robust body of research. Studies exploring people's experience of hand loss or serious impairment, for instance, commonly cite the far-reaching economic, social, and emotional challenges such events can precipitate. Among them, occupational changes necessitated by disability within a work environment designed for typical hands; social stigma in a culture where the word *typical* has come to mean "correct"; and injury to a sense of self bound up with hands' appearance and the independence they enable. Anxiety or mood disorders may also result.

Thus, in continual service both physically and psychosocially, hands become an integral part of who we are, with the power to influence self-regard and others. Considering this, one can appreciate why Clint Hallam struggled to accept a donor hand that served him so poorly across dimensions. His is not everyone's experience, though; many people adapt and thrive in changed bodies, and in chapter 14, I'll touch on the role of OT in that process.

Still, surgeons encountering a severely injured hand today will do everything they can to preserve both function and form. In doing so, they'll pay particular attention to peripheral nerves, knowing the devastating impact of lost motor and sensory function, and that even sensory impairment alone can cause difficulties. If you are typically handed and want to better appreciate these facts, consider turning your bedtime routine into an experiment tonight. Using just one hand (and no cheeky assists from cohabitants), strip off your street clothes, return them to their drawers and closets, and don your pajamas.

If you're really keen, next put on a pair of gloves and complete the rest of your routine, two-handed—makeup and contact lens removal, face-washing, toothbrushing, whatever your usual drill. Throughout, notice what's harder to do and what's not, what adaptations you make to compensate for your temporary impairment, what goes wrong, and how long everything takes relative to your usual pace. Afterward, were you more aware of all that your hands, and particularly their sensations, enable you to do?

My awakening to that effect began in the ambulance on the night of my accident, when I had the ghastly impression of sensibility itself draining out of my right hand. At first, the hand had felt like it always did when inactive and unstimulated: unfeeling, yet having a feel *to it* that told me it was there and part of me, even when I wasn't looking at it. But over the course of the ride, that sense of "thereness," or embodiment, receded steadily from fingertips, to knuckles, to the heel of my hand, and into my wrist, where the median nerve serving it had been transected. It was as if my hand had disappeared somewhere between Brooklyn and Bellevue, except that it remained in plain sight. Out of sight, my body was preparing for peripheral nerve regeneration.

As a refresher, a nerve is a bundle of axons. An axon is the stemlike part of a neuron, and individual axons are ensheathed in Schwann cells, plus an outer layer of connective tissue. The axons in peripheral nerves stretch from neuron cell bodies in, or near, the spinal cord to specific sites in the skin, muscles, or organs. There, the axons' branched endings communicate with target cells, either to transmit central nervous system commands to muscles, or to relay data about the body's environment to the central nervous system to inform those commands.

Upon transection of my median nerve, part of this feedback loop was broken, causing loss of motor and sensory function in much of my hand. The regeneration program would attempt to restore it by extending the live axon segments—those above the wound, thus still connected to their cell bodies—across the wound to their original targets in my hand. (Because this program operates on the level of the axon, not the entire nerve, I'll refer to it as *peripheral axon regeneration* from here on out.)

To clear the path for regenerating axons, the dead axon segments (those stretching from the wound into the hand, thus cut off from their cell bodies) disintegrate in spectacular, instantaneous bursts, leaving their Schwann cell and connective tissue sheaths behind. Taking charge of the scene like the Red Cross in a natural disaster, these Schwann cells recruit immune cells to help consume debris from the disintegrated axons and other tissues damaged in the accident, and to kill pathogens that may have entered the body through the wound. They also flood the area with proteins that will instruct participating cells in their roles in regeneration.

Meanwhile, the cell bodies shift from transmission to growth mode, churning out protein building blocks for their axon extensions. These will give the extensions a stringy, stretchy form and, at their tips, a growth cone, which one neuroscientist I interviewed vividly described as a "grippy hand" for the way it propels a regenerating axon forward, adhering to, then pushing off of, cells along its path.

Within days of transection, cleanup is usually complete, and axon regeneration begins. The live axon segments sprout their growth cones, which reach across the wound to begin the journey toward their targets in the hand, via the connective tissue sheaths abandoned by the disintegrated axon segments. Concurrently, Schwann cells in the axon sheaths reorganize themselves to provide the growth cones with nutrients and a "sticky" surface they can easily grasp along the way. To help keep them on track, the Schwann cells also secrete proteins as beacons, and the growth cones continually repoint themselves toward the areas of highest protein concentration. If enough axons reach their targets in the hand and reestablish communication with the central nervous system, some motor and sensory function may be restored.

Any step of the process can go wrong, however, and regularly does. The live axons might fail to cross the wound site, despite surgeons' providing them a bridge—via nerve sheath repair (as in my case, when the gap to be crossed is relatively small) or nerve graft (when the gap is large). They might be blocked by scar tissue or lingering cellular debris. Growth cones can veer off course, despite the Schwann cell protein beacons. If an axon's progress is too slow, Schwann cells may not be able to nourish and guide it for the duration of its journey, or its target cell may die for lack of innervation before the axon arrives. Finally, the body's immune response to injury could fail, allowing infection to take hold; or the immune response could persist too long, thus inflicting dangerous amounts of "bystander damage" (killing off healthy cells as well as pathogens).

It seems a miracle, then, that peripheral axon regeneration ever proceeds as "designed," and given this, I wondered about my future hand the same way parents-to-be might wonder about their future child: Will it be healthy and capable? What will it look like? Will it feel part of me? How will it change me, and my life?

It would be months before I had even an inkling of the answers, since peripheral axons grow an average of about a millimeter per day under the best of conditions, and mine had up to twenty-four centimeters to cover. In the meantime, I could do nothing to promote healthy regeneration beyond eating and sleeping well and taking my prescribed antibiotics. This was nature's stretch of the three-legged race to restore my hand function, and she would dictate the pace and quality of performance. Though accepting that fact felt acutely unnatural.

13

Farewell to the Dream Team

The morning after flying home from Nashville, I awake in my empty apartment feeling like an imposter spying on my former life. Before the accident, despite a hyperactive social life, I have almost always been alone when at home, contentedly whiling away the hours reading and listening to music in my living room, talking to friends on the phone while cooking dinner in my tiny but efficient kitchen, watching a bit of TV in bed before sleeping. So there's nothing obviously amiss with my solitude here. But having been in the company of family around the clock since the accident, I now find the silence weighty and foreboding.

Alert to the dangers of dwelling too much on it, I steer my thoughts to the more pleasant prospect of my appointment with Dr. Vargas and team that morning. I am keen for their view on my progress, which I suspect will be positive, and don't want to be late. I hurry out of bed, knowing it will take twice as long to get out the door without someone to count pills, make breakfast, and call the car service while I bathe and dress.

I arrive at the hospital lobby by 7:30 a.m. to secure a place at the head of the long line for the elevator to the Adult Musculoskeletal Clinics, the various corridors of examination rooms clustered by specialty (hand, ortho, arthritis), where surgeons follow up with their patients on an outpatient basis following surgery. While all patients technically have a specific appointment time (mine is 8:30 a.m.), they are nonetheless called in roughly first-come, first-served order. Also, appointments get pushed back by as much as two hours over the course of the day as surgeons squeeze in emergency cases, so savvy patients wrangle early time slots and arrive well ahead of them.

At 8:00 a.m., a stern security guard who's been blocking the elevator steps aside and motions the queuing patients forward. We surge toward the elevator on crutches, and in wheelchairs, splints, and slings, with the stony determination of Manhattan commuters pushing onto the 4 train at rush hour. Holding my hand a little higher than usual, I chuckle at the crazy scene, confident that people will take care not to jostle me as long as they can see my swaddled limb. My faith on this point proves misplaced, but I am at least glad to see the nonambulatory among the crowd given some consideration.

The elevator doors open onto the second floor and we pour out the door, limping, wheeling, and shuffling to line up again at the registration counters for our respective clinics. Thanks to my early arrival, I win second place in line at the hand clinic. I dig my red clinic card and appointment confirmation sheet out of my urban survival pack—the boho embroidery bag I wear crossways over my chest.

In addition to wallet and cell phone, it holds a novel to entertain me during long waits at the hospital, pen and notepad to record medical questions and exercises performed, cocoa-butter lotion for massaging my scar, a couple of doses of all my meds, a small bottle of water and energy bar with which to take them, a tube of lip gloss, and usually some insurance documentation to mail or verify with the Bellevue finance office.

The bag is hideous, but big enough for me to easily sling on and off over my splint, and not the worst of my many concessions to function over fashion in the wake of the accident. Others include a pair of perilously-close-to-orthopedic Velcro-closure shoes, a coat whose right sleeve Mom slit open to accommodate my splint, and three dark, long-sleeved jersey shirts with hugely stretched-out right arms, which altogether constitute my entire wardrobe for the moment. Erica says I look great in my skinny jeans, though, so at least the Bellevue diet of trauma and drugs is working for me.

"Rebecca Fogg," I say, placing my plastic clinic identification card and appointment slip on the counter in front of the clerk. I smile brightly, partly because I am, ironically, always happy to be at clinic, and partly to ward off the bad administrative juju that sometimes afflicts people dependent on big bureaucracies. Like when the computer system doesn't reflect your last several hundred dollars of payments, causing the clerk to insist you must pay out of pocket for an appointment because you haven't met your insurance deductible, though in fact you have.

"I know, Miss Fogg!" the clerk exclaims. "You're the one who came in with all your family that one time, right?" I nod. "That's so nice. Not a lot of people have family like that. How y'doing?" She smiles back at me as she embosses my appointment slip with my card and places the former in a file for Dr. Vargas.

"Much better, thanks."

"Well, you take care now."

"Thanks, you too."

A lot of people wouldn't believe me if I told them these kinds of interactions happen all the time—strangers seeing me in pain, wanting me to feel better and telling me so. But they do, and they make me kvell over my fellow New Yorkers, especially when they happen at Bellevue. In her role as bouncer here at Club Miserable, this clerk sees the gamut of human circumstances every day, mostly ranging from unlucky to abominable. She also probably endures some seriously testy treatment from scared, exhausted, and frustrated patients; and if not for my opioid-induced calm, I might be one of the guilty. So when she smiles brightly, remembers my family, and wishes me well, I couldn't feel more blessed if the Dalai Lama himself were to meditate for my well-being.

I make a beeline for my favorite seat in the waiting room,

near the doorway where the clerks none too loudly summon patients by name, so that I don't miss my cue. Patients who don't respond promptly essentially end up on standby for an appointment, and can expect a good long wait before the over-booked doctors manage to squeeze them in. I remove my splint in preparation for a round of hand exercises, having learned that the only way to get through all the prescribed daily repetitions, plus massage and splint washing, is to make them the priority activity for any waking moment in which my left hand isn't needed for eating or grooming. All other busi-ness or pleasure has to come second, otherwise I end up sitting in bed late at night, worn out and fighting sleep and anxiety to finish the last few rounds.

As patients begin to arrive in a steady stream, we regulars in the Upper Extremity Occupational Therapy Room recog-nize and greet each other. A middle-aged woman spotting me from across the room smiles, then raises her brows and points to my hand. Each week she brings her elderly father to therapy, along with her young son. The son plays contentedly with his toy dinosaurs for the duration of each appointment, utterly unfazed by the physical deformities surrounding him. I don't speak Chinese and the woman doesn't speak English, but I easily understand her "How's the bum hand?" gesture, and reciprocate with a "Doing well, thanks" smile and "What about your dad?" nod. Good, he's doing better.

Then I quickly exchange statuses with Kelly, a Good Sa-maritan whose reward for trying to separate a couple of scuf-fling dogs had been a big bite into her little finger, as she edges past me to take a seat in the back of the waiting room. She and I clicked immediately when we met, and when we are occasionally assigned to neighboring examination rooms at clinic we hang out in the hallway, happily kibitzing until some nurse shoos us back into our respective rooms to await our physicians.

Next, I welcome a guy named Mike as he sidles into the seat next to me. Having long since revealed the causes of our sorry accidents to each other (his hand was macerated by a slamming steel door), we launch into an entertaining round of Who's Your Favorite Doc? I feel mildly treacherous for having gossiped about my dream team, then cut myself some slack. It wasn't admirable behavior, but it wasn't malicious, either—and it felt nice to have a carefree laugh with a fellow patient.

At 9:30 a.m., a dreadlocked, Rasta-capped clerk in a wheelchair escorts me back to one of the hand clinic's eight small, white examination rooms. Perched on the exam table, I am no more than a few pages into my novel when a resident walks in. I'm disappointed, first because he isn't Dr. Vargas, though that isn't especially surprising, since the chief resident is rarely the first one through the door; second, because he isn't Dr. Matthews. In fact, I don't recognize this guy at all. Given Bellevue's function as a teaching hospital, residents not involved in my case often examine me as a learning opportunity. But if that's his deal, it's unusual for him to be here without one of my team.

The resident nods hello as he passes me to take a seat at the desktop computer. "How've you been doing?" he asks, as if he knows me.

"Very well, thanks," I respond distractedly. Have I gotten the appointment time wrong? Have I missed my team's last day?

He pulls up my record on-screen and scrolls through it. "How's the pain?" This is the first of a number of routine questions designed to flag potential concerns. I respond that the pain has been lessening, though I still require hydrocodone around the clock, which he deems normal.

"Would you like me to tell you everything that was severed and repaired, Dr. . . . ?" I ask, believing I need to orient him to my injury and repair. Otherwise he'll need to scroll all the way back to the first entry in my record to acquire this essential information.

"Ed. Ed Espinoza. Thanks, but I'm all up to speed. I actually participated in your surgery," he responds.

"Oh, I'm so sorry! Thank you for everything . . . I . . . didn't remember you."

"That's OK." He smiles. "You had a big team. We never actually met." I want to know who else I've neglected to appreciate, but I have too many burning questions to cover in this brief appointment to waste a proverbial bullet on that one.

Dr. Espinoza asks a few more routine questions, pecking at the computer keyboard as I answer. He knows what he's doing, but we have no history with each other. So I hold my questions for . . . whichever familiar guy shows up. Then he rises from the computer and steps in front of me. Wait—he's going to do the physical exam, too? Where's my dream team? I hold out my hand and he begins to tear apart the Velcro strips that hold the splint to my hand, very slowly as if trying not to make any noise, though I guess he's just taking care not to hurt me.

"Here," I say, waving his hand away and ripping the strips apart in quick succession—one, two, three, four, five—freeing my hand of the splint with the confidence of a veteran parent extricating a toddler from a poopy diaper. I've come a long way on this skill myself.

"Show-off!" he quips good-naturedly, if a bit sheepishly. I have embarrassed him and feel a frisson of shame.

"Hey, kiddo! How's the hand?" Dr. Matthews bounds through the doorway, smiling and shaking my left hand with his. He reminds me of the heavyweight rowers on my college crew team: big and affable, made winning look easy.

"Hey! Hand is good," I reply, instantly matching his energy and cheer. Dr. Espinoza steps aside without a word, allowing the more senior Dr. Matthews to take over the physical exam. "OK, I've got to ask . . . did you ever row crew?"

"Yes, I did," Dr. Matthews says, nodding and chuckling, I suppose at the unlikeliness of this fact surfacing in a medical context. "You?"

As we fall into easy rowing banter, I feel another twinge of guilt about Dr. Espinoza. Is it obvious he isn't in my Favorite Docs Club? But it passes quickly. If he's noticed my greater ease with Dr. Matthews, he won't be offended. He's a professional and will be glad I'm feeling comfortable.

Dr. Matthews holds my wrist lightly in his left palm and places the tips of his right index and middle fingers just above the scar, where the live segment of the transected nerve still functions, and begins tapping lightly toward my hand. I can feel his touch on the surface of my skin above the scar, but not below it, where the dead segment of the nerve has disintegrated. However, *inside* my wrist, beneath that numb patch of skin, his taps set off what feel like tiny explosions.

"You feel anything there?" he asks.

"Yeah . . . I mean, sort of." I envision golden fireworks, flaring and dying in succession against the red-brown muck of my muscles, and search for words to describe the sensation. "Not on the skin, that's totally numb. But . . . inside my wrist . . . sparks, tingling, wherever you tap."

"That's good. That means the live end of the transected nerve is regrowing," he responds. "It's called the Tinel sign."

How auspicious. And what a simple means of measuring the progress of the all-important nerve, one I can use myself. I scrawl *Tinel* in my notebook and look forward to Googling the term when I get home.

"Where does it stop?" he asks, continuing to tap into my hand along the path of the severed nerve.

"Here," I point, about an inch below my wrist crease. "How long will it take for the nerve to grow all the way back?"

"Everyone's different; there's no set pace. But on average

you can assume it takes a couple weeks after repair to start growing, then it can grow about a millimeter a day. In that case, you're right on track: your repair was about a month ago, and the nerve has covered fifteen millimeters."

Suddenly there's another pair of hands in the mix. Dr. Vargas has slipped into the room, just when I've given up on seeing him. Gratitude, a long-suppressed yearning for good news, and the desire for his esteem well up in me, and I greet him with the warmth of an old friend, which in my mind, he is. Does that make me a cliché, the idolizing patient? Probably. Doesn't matter. Inspiration, in any form, will speed my recovery. I figure the end justifies the means.

"All right. Let's have a look," he says as Dr. Matthews cedes his place in front of me. Dr. Vargas reaches his hands nearer, palms open upward. In opera the gesture would represent a tormented soprano's plea for mercy from a bitter lover or punishing god. Here in clinic, it is how every medical professional I encounter beckons for my right hand, answering my unspoken call for help.

You can't ignore hands that are touching you, so at this point I know Dr. Vargas's almost as well as he knows mine: larger even than my wide-reaching instrumentalist's hands; lightly freckled; the archetypal surgeon's slender fingers, finished off with close-cropped, oval fingernails. Unhesitating and deft, they speak of his insight and determination when he is silent.

Dr. Vargas examines the knitting wound, repeats the Tinel

test, and notes the color throughout my hand, then delivers the happy verdict: good progress, with blood flow adequate despite closure of the severed artery, and the hopeful signs of nerve regeneration prickling and tingling in all the right places. Next, he grips my fingers—still frozen at a ninety-degree angle to my palm—and slowly pulls them back toward him about a half an inch, to stretch out the repaired tendons, which scar tissue and disuse have rendered inelastic. It feels like he's pulling my hand off, yanking the muscles and tendons out of my arm like meat from a lobster claw. The pain is almost as bad as the intense burning I felt in the hospital after the accident. I paste a neutral expression on my face to mask my reaction because, like any self-respecting former college athlete, I know that the only thing worse than feeling pain is admitting to feeling it.

"Does that hurt?" he asks.

"A little," I answer.

Dr. Vargas pulls my fingers back a quarter inch more. I envision my tendons snapping, curling up, and retracting like broken guitar strings. The fear of rupture intensifies my pain, but I trust Dr. Vargas, so rightly or wrongly, I don't protest. I do, however, appreciate the distraction of Dr. Matthews's conversation.

"You know this is our last day in Plastics Clinic, right?"

"Yeah, I know. I'm really going to miss you guys," I reply. "Where do you all go from here?"

As Drs. Matthews and Espinoza excitedly tell me about

their next posts, Dr. Vargas continues to inflict pain in opening my hand. Without looking up, he says, "I'll be filling in for my successor here in a couple months. You could make an appointment to see me then."

"Thank you so much . . . I will definitely do that," I say. "Consistency really means a lot to me these days."

He looks up at me with a nearly imperceptible smile. "It's as much for me as it is for you. I want to know how you're doing."

14

It's All Up to You, Kiddo: Rehabilitating a Replanted Hand

I knew I was going to like my new high school violin teacher, Connie, when she sent me home ten minutes into my third lesson. It was the early 1980s, my family had just moved from upstate New York to Nashville, Tennessee, and the transition to a community whose culture I initially found inscrutable and exclusionary was tough. Missing old friends, striving to make new ones, and consumed by a heavier-than-required course load (my ticket back north to college), I just hadn't gotten around to picking up the violin that particular week.

So when Connie asked me to play the first movement of the concerto I was working on, I did what I'd often done in middle school lessons—kept mum about my lack of practice and played the piece through, paying close attention to the suggested improvements my teacher had written on my music the prior week. I took no pride in this deception, but it had never failed to impress other teachers, and I'd consistently won honors for my efforts. The last note still ringing, I brought my bow arm down and looked expectantly at Connie.

"Sounds like you haven't had much chance to practice," she said, "so I think it would be best if we picked this up next week."

My body went cold. She meant just this piece, right? "Uh, yeah. OK . . . do you want to hear the étude?"

"Have you spent any more time on that?"

"Not really . . ." I felt faint.

"Let's leave it here, then. I'll see you next week."

And then, because I was still too young to drive, I slunk out of her studio and sat on the curb of the music school driveway for forty-five minutes until my mother arrived to pick me up. No way was I going to go to the school office to ask to use a phone to tell her she had to pick me up early because I'd shamed myself and my family by not practicing enough for my lesson. Mom was going to hear that the lesson had gone "fine." Beneath the shame, though, a sense of excitement was emerging. Connie expected more of me than other teachers had, which must mean she saw more potential in me than they had or, at least, cared enough to hold me to a higher standard. That felt good. I knew I could achieve more, too, and wanted to. I came from a musical family. Music had spoken to me from a young age, and I needed more language—that language—to express myself. Music was understanding, belonging.

Violin became the consuming occupation of my teenage years, and the gateway to numerous firsts: first encounters with Bartók and Barber, two of my great musical loves; first barely supervised living experience (at an international summer music school); first non-American friends; first kiss, first snog. So intimate was my relationship with the instrument that, hauling it across town and country, I'd find myself absentmindedly patting its case. And sometimes, when I suffered in real life, my violin suffered violence or neglect in my dreams.

I quit playing violin after my first year of college—a rash response to an overwhelming mix of insecurity about my talent, poor chemistry with my new teacher, and frustration at missing out on a lot of campus life due to practice and rehearsals. I felt guilt and dread instead of joy when picking up my violin, and I couldn't see any way forward with it. I didn't tell anyone how I felt, not even Connie. There's no point, I'd thought; I just have to be an adult and make the tough decision. I found the activities I subsequently threw myself into— crew, musical theater, an a cappella singing group—rewarding. But the silence of the instrument lurking under my bed, and the perceived waste of my investment in learning it, nagged at me for decades.

Learning an instrument is embodying it—training your brain to understand its form, feel, and feedback so well that you know how to operate it as if it were part of you. It's also developing the physical fitness and skill to execute the required moves, because knowing how to do something isn't the same as being able to do it. This is exactly the kind of work that lay before me in OT, six weeks after the accident. The swollen, scaly appendage attached to my right arm wasn't *my* hand; mine had been a perfectly calibrated system that continuously whispered to me about the physical world and automatically shaped itself to my intent. This one was dead silent, immobile, blooming with obstructive scar tissue, lacking one tendon and nursing repairs to many others.

First, my brain had to learn how to instruct it—and its tissues made fit to comply—to the extent possible, since there was no doubt that I'd sustain some degree of permanent impairment. Then Beth and I would have to figure out how I could improvise around my hand's deficits to perform important tasks, how I could change the way I interacted with the built world so that my impairment did not cause disability. The distinction between impairment and disability was new to me, but immediately resonated. Efficacy is the product of performance and context, not an intrinsic quality of the performer; an impaired hand can be highly useful, just as a technically flawed musical performance can be deeply moving.

That first stage of rehabilitation requires what I'd call *practicing*, but which some scientists more engagingly call *motor babbling*, after the vocal babbling babies do to learn language so that they can ask for what they need. Both kinds of babble activate that central/peripheral nervous system feedback loop I first mentioned in chapter 2, which enables us to respond appropriately to our changing internal and external environments.

For example, a vocal-babbling baby attempts to mimic the words of her doting dad, and knows she's finally got one right when she hears herself produce the matching sound and Dad beams with delight. In motor babbling with my violin, say I want to play a C. I place my left middle finger on the A string. When a C-sharp rings out instead of a C, I know that next time, I need to place that finger lower on the string. I try again and again until I learn exactly where to place the finger on the string to hit a C, and have developed the dexterity to reliably do so.

After massive amounts of such babbling, I get very good at predicting what will happen when I act on my violin in any particular way, so I usually know how to achieve a desired result. When I do make mistakes, I quickly recognize and know how to correct them, and eventually, the basic mechanics of playing become automatic. The violin feels like a part of me, and I can turn my focus to the musical interpretation of a piece.

How does motor babbling achieve this? You may recall from chapter 2 how the brain shapes our experience, for instance by automatically coordinating our initial response to survival threats. Our experience also shapes the brain, causing widespread alterations in structure and function. The brain's capacity for such change is commonly called *neuroplasticity*, and motor babbling leverages it to our advantage. Specifically, extensive repetition of an activity signals to the brain that the data streams associated with it are important. So the brain allocates more of its capacity to their processing, and involved neurons undergo physical and chemical changes that strengthen communication among them. The result is higher sensitivity to, and more effective use of, the data, thus better performance of the activities depending on it.

Functional images of string players' brains suggest this phenomenon at work. A well-known study showed a larger share of processing capacity devoted to data from the players' left fingers, which are constantly engaged in fine motor movements while playing, than data from their right fingers, which are relatively less active in controlling the bow. The string players' left-finger processing capacity also exceeded that of nonmusicians in the study.

Repetition alone doesn't lead to proficiency, though, as anyone forced to play literally any sport with me in school gym class could tell you. Studies suggest that you have to *want* to improve, whether for satisfaction, survival, or some other personally meaningful payoff. Also, you need to know which movements to repeat to achieve desired results.

Studying violin with Connie, I learned to home in on the smallest, most troublesome fragments of a piece—a convoluted run of notes or an awkward string-crossing—and experiment with different approaches to learning them. Sometimes the best approach is obvious, like practicing a fast section slowly until you can play it all the way through correctly, then gradually increasing the speed.

Other approaches are counterintuitive. For instance, to play a fast, even rhythm (da da da da) *perfectly* evenly, Connie suggested I practice it in every possible *uneven* rhythm (DA da DA da . . . da DA da DA . . . DA da da da . . . da da da DA . . . and so on). Then, magically, it felt easy to play the notes evenly. Little by little, through such practice tricks, technique drills, and discipline, a musician's mastery expands from fragments to measures to phrases to pages, and from technical accuracy to compelling expression.

In OT, too, you break the big performance goals—self-care, work, meaningful pastimes—down into their smallest motor components, and work on each until you master it. Then you gradually string the components together until you're reaching, grasping, pinching, and placing as best you can. If you think of grasping with your right hand, for instance, you can see that it requires curling every joint of every digit in toward the palm, on a trajectory that leaves sufficient space between digits and palm for the object you want to grasp. My exercise goals thus progressed over several months, from flattening out my hand (which was frozen with fingers ninety degrees to palm after long immobilization to protect healing tendons), to regaining range of motion in every joint of every digit, to moving the digits in a fluid and coordinated fashion, and, finally, attempting useful tasks.

That wouldn't be the exercise arc for every spaghetti wrist case, though. An effective OT regimen takes into account the fact that every injury, and therefore every surgical repair, is unique—as are the biological, psychological, and environmental circumstances that influence our individual responses to injury and rehabilitation (just as they do in our individual experiences of pain and responses to trauma). We scar in different ways and heal at different rates, for instance, and we don't always have the time, understanding, and/or confidence to fully engage with the rehabilitation process. Therefore, there was no off-the-shelf OT program that would address my specific circumstances; Beth had to design one using evidence-based guidelines for related injuries and her own clinical experience.

She essentially had just two mechanisms to leverage in doing so: motion and force. Motion stretches out joints, ligaments, and tendons stiff from disuse. It also helps prevent scar tissue from accumulating in the wrong places, by creating friction between surfaces, thus dislodging scar-tissue cells before they take root. Motion can be passive (for instance, my healthy left hand moving my impaired right hand) or active (my impaired right hand moving on its own). Force is the transference of energy from muscles to tendons that takes place during active motion. While any active motion "loads" tendons with some degree of force, more aggressive active motion—like squeezing, pressing, and lifting—loads more.

Striking the right balance between motion and force is tricky, with serious consequences for getting it wrong. Beth had to assign exercises that would load my tendons with just enough force to pull through obstructive scarring—essential because, as Beth liked to say, a tendon trying to glide against scarred tissue is like an ice-skater trying to skate through wet cement—but not so much as to rupture the tendon repairs. To complicate matters, key outcome drivers—how well *my* body would heal, how much force *my* healing tendons could bear, how well *I* would adhere to the exercise regime—were unknowable, at least initially. So Beth would have to start with estimates. She'd also have to account for the unusual extent of my injury, and the strength of Dr. Vargas's repair, which was a function of the number and location of sutures he'd placed in the tendons.

The solution? An adaptive algorithm hinging on one factor Beth could objectively measure: lag. If you consider that healthy digits describe a (roughly) 180-degree arc when closing from a flat hand into a flat-fingered fist, lag tells you the portion of that arc that an impaired hand must regain in active range, through therapy. Beth calculated this by subtracting my impaired hand's active range of motion from its passive range of motion. Authors of the algorithm suggested that if active motion lags passive motion by fifteen degrees or more, healing flexor tendons are stuck in scar tissue, and more force must be applied to break them free of it. They also defined a pyramid of exercises that loads increasing amounts of force onto the tendons.

The bigger the lag and the longer it persists, the higher up the force-loading pyramid you go. If you reach the top of the pyramid and still have a big lag, you're looking at surgery to scrape out the scar tissue that exercises won't budge. My lag started at 130 degrees, so darned if I didn't have to climb all the way to the top of that bloody pyramid *and* spend time in a splint that stretched my repaired tendons so painfully hard that I threw it against my bedroom wall after the first ninety minutes. "*Tons* of wounds, *tons* of scar tissue," Beth said in one of our interviews for this book. But under her careful supervision I pushed through it all, and can now fist-bump with the best of them.

If you've ever managed through an extensive rehabilitation program, then you know that it is psychologically, as well as physically, demanding. If you haven't, imagine you're a regular in Bellevue's Upper Extremity Occupational Therapy Room, with an injury like mine. Your wounded appendage already hurts because it's inflamed, and because your central nervous system is freaking out over the garbled data it's getting from the transected peripheral nerve. Still, you have to pull and push it in directions it doesn't want to go, which makes it hurt more. Inflicting pain on yourself is not a skill that comes naturally, and it takes an unusual kind of discipline to override instinctual objections to it.

Pain aside, the exercises are intensely frustrating. There you are, ferociously concentrating on a motor task that, for as long as you can remember, you've never had to think about, and you're apparently getting nowhere with it. The frustration would be easier to bear if the goal were positive, but alas, you're not acquiring some intriguing skill that will unlock wonderful new experiences. You're busting butt for a result somewhere between dysfunctional and suboptimal, and you don't know whether your permanent impairment will be disabling or merely annoying.

The practicalities of rehab—keeping the ever-changing exercise regimen straight, scheduling and commuting to appointments, processing health insurance claims (if you're fortunate enough to have health insurance)—impose stress. And you're grappling with all of the above while in an opioid haze and struggling with self-care. In short, rehabilitation demands maximum inner resources, just when you have the least to invest. But somehow, you rise to the challenge.

Everything that helped me cope with the psychological distress of my accident—loved ones, studying science, etc.—also helped me meet the demands of OT. The sense of achievement I derived from performing my OT exercises further fueled my motivation, as did my confidence in the process, predicated on years of violin practice, which had proved how thousands of tiny, isolated movements could add up to an expansive repertoire of fluid, powerful movement. And Beth was just the right teacher for me—talented, attuned to my particular needs, compassionate yet demanding. She was a straight talker, too, who never pretended certainty to encourage me or avoid difficult conversations. If she had dished out a single "You got this!" I'd have doubted everything else she said.

In the best-case scenario, OT results in a body that can do whatever an individual deems necessary and meaningful, and can yield intangible benefits, too. Ability is not a fixed thing, because our bodies, our environment, and what we need and want to do with them change throughout our lives. In its emphasis on adaptation and ends over means, then, OT can prepare people to navigate undesired physical challenges with realistic hope and creativity, and to bear the emotional sense of loss associated with former physical abilities. I didn't fully appreciate this until I had a violin lesson with Connie in late 2006.

By October of that year, I had returned to work and completed my course of OT, having regained the function I needed to perform important daily activities. And while sensibility in my repaired hand was poor, it didn't seem to be holding me back in any serious way. Still, I worried. What if my sensory deficit prevented me from engaging in some meaningful activity I hadn't yet considered? Was there anything I could be doing to prevent that scenario, and the accompanying heartache? I didn't want to end up like my friend Maggie with the broken wrist, wishing I'd worked harder at recovery.

I dove down a Google hole in pursuit of answers, and even consulted a couple of specialist hand surgeons and therapists. But what I learned was either ambiguous or flat-out discouraging, and this posed a dilemma: Do I continue to invest time, money, and emotional bandwidth trying to beat the odds? Or do I just accept my right hand as it is? I feared regretting the latter. But I was so very tired of working in pursuit of uncertain benefits.

Driven by the same kind of sick, self-defeating curiosity that makes you pick at a scab, I pulled my violin case out from under the bed one day and guiltily swept a path through the thick layer of dust that had accumulated on its canvas cover. Autopilot took over, and I opened the cover and unlatched the hard plastic case beneath with a familiar *snap, zip, zip, clotch, clotch* that made me smile. I fitted the shoulder rest to the instrument and tucked it between my left shoulder and jaw, picked up my bow and tightened the bow hair, tuned the violin strings, and endeavored a scale. Two strokes in, I lost my grip on the bow and dropped it—something I'd never done, even as a child. I attempted the scale again, then some easy bits of a concerto, with the same result. I took this as a sign that my hopes of improved hand function were futile, and reinterred my violin.

I couldn't forget the episode, though, or the dilemma that had prompted it. So when I visited Nashville for Christmas 2006, I asked Connie if we could have a lesson instead of our usual lunch date. I told her I wanted her to observe my bow grip so she could discern the error of position or motion that caused me to drop the bow. But what I really wanted was for her to agree that playing with my impaired hand was a lost cause. Then I could abandon that long-nagging dream of resuming violin without "being a quitter," and stop chasing elixirs for hand dysfunction and regret.

I insisted on taking the lesson sitting on the edge of her bed, rather than standing, because Connie was going to let me play her exquisite, centuries-old violin, an honor she'd periodically bestowed on me in our younger years. Before I picked up the instrument, she reached toward me with her long, angular hands, palms open upward, beckoning for my right hand the same way my surgeons always did.

I extended it to her, palm down. She cradled it at the wrist with her right hand and cupped my fingertips in her left. "Now let your hand hang heavy. I've got it, you can let go. Good." Her gently husky voice, imbued with empathy and confidence, had soothed a great deal of my teenage angst, and still reassured. "Feel that?" she said, alternately bouncing my wrist and jiggling my fingers. "That's how loose it should feel when you're playing." I felt the looseness, and it felt good—a novel experience for my "new" hand, whose numbness often made it feel stiff.

Next, she threaded the frog of her bow (the rectangular piece securing the horsehair to the stick) between my fingers and thumb, inviting me to grasp it and take a few strokes on her violin. I nestled the instrument between my left shoulder and jaw, and slowly drew the bow back and forth across the D string. I managed three strokes before my grip collapsed, and the bow slid through my closed hand onto her bed. "See?" I exclaimed, petulant.

Her eyes told me we were not finished, so I picked up the bow again. Tucking a thick lock of brown-gray hair behind her ear, she leaned in to assess the placement of every finger, while I recited my hand's deficits: the atrophied thumb, which couldn't properly oppose my fingers on top of the stick; my unfeeling first three digits, which couldn't adjust to the moving bow; and my little finger, which, perhaps due to an irreparable transected tendon, couldn't maintain its footing on the end of the stick.

"Hmm . . ." Connie said, studying my hand on the bow. "Keep your fingers on the bow, but let go of the weight. I'll hold it in place." She jiggled the bow in my hand, illustrating the flexibility that was my goal. "Now . . . what happens if you put your thumb here?" she said, tapping the bottom of the frog. Normally the thumb was tucked under the stick, braced between it and a nook carved out of the top of the frog.

"*There?*"

"Sure," she said, continuing to explain that the bow grip she and I had learned was the one advocated by Ivan Galamian, a twentieth-century master of the instrument. But violinists had always adapted technique to their unique style and anatomy, from classical legend Jascha Heifetz and his flat-fingered "Russian" hold, to country music virtuoso Mark O'Connor and his thumb-under-frog grip, which Connie had just suggested for me. "I knew a kid at music camp who had six fingers," she said. "Obviously he couldn't hold the bow the same way I did, but he figured out what worked for him. And he was *good.*"

I gave the grip a try. It felt more solid, as my thumb had more purchase on the bottom of the frog, so I could press the stick more firmly against my index finger on top of the stick. "Huh," I said.

"Holding it that way, can you bounce your wrist?" I could. "Great. And the fingers . . . can they move with the bow, without dropping it?"

I took a few strokes in the new grip. I couldn't quite strike the requisite balance between firmness and flexibility, but it seemed attainable with practice, and Connie recommended some exercises toward that end. She also suggested constructing a "pinky house"—a popular practice aid for beginning violinists consisting of a divot at the end of the bow where one can lodge the little finger to keep it from slipping. A corn pad usually does the trick. All my objections deftly countered, the ball was now in my court. I handed Connie's violin and bow back to her.

"You know," she said, returning them to their case, "you don't have to play what you used to play. You don't even have to play violin music. Play anything you like. Just *play*." I thought of my favorite songs by Barber and Fauré and felt a hunger in my hands that I hadn't for many years. Quietly, because I thought my voice might break, I thanked Connie for her help.

She smiled, turning her hazel eyes to mine. "Only problem was, you thought there was a right way to play."

15

Rotas and Meltdowns

A couple of weeks after bidding the dream team farewell in late February 2006, I'm obsessing about my new job (on top of everything else), though that's nothing new. In seven years with the same global financial services company, I've held six jobs at three levels, in five functions, four departments, and three divisions. Officially, the jobs variously entailed consumer marketing, customer servicing, business-to-business sales, business development, and technology implementation. Fundamentally, all the work was, and is, the same: Know where the business needs to go. Pinpoint the problems and opportunities you can tackle to get there, given the time you've got and the resources you can wrangle. Craft explicit plans for doing so, enable and inspire everyone you can to support the plans, and adjust them along the way as needed.

A love of learning, thirst for achievement, and near-pathological drive for financial security have kept me moving at this breathless pace, as have the company's frequent reorganizations and intensely competitive "up or out" culture. And there's no lull in the hustle when one assumes a new role because, as one boss told me, "It takes six months to learn a job, but you've got to prove yourself in three."

That's why, at 11:00 a.m. on a Wednesday, I'm sitting at my dinner table, right elbow propped to keep my splinted hand elevated, with four résumés, a spiral notebook, and a blue ballpoint pen fanned out in front of me. I'd risen several hours earlier to allow time for one-handed bathing, dressing, breakfasting, splint washing, and dispensing of pills for the day—and to perform one hundred of my three hundred daily hand exercise reps. Now I really need to be napping. Instead, I'm preparing to conduct final-round interviews for two open positions on my new team.

I had posted the positions internally just before my accident, and they attracted scores of applicants, each of whom needed to be ranked and either interviewed or politely rejected, before the finalists could be identified. I wouldn't normally have outsourced management of this process. But my new colleagues generously offered their help, I desperately need it, and I trust them. So I let them whittle the applicant pool down to a long list of serious contenders, interview the first-round candidates I selected from it, and pass me two excellent finalists for each job.

Studying their résumés awakens my excitement about my new department's charter to develop new revenue streams for the company, and the small team I might build to pursue it with me. Job offers, strong performance reviews, and promotions are exciting, too, but my highest professional highs have involved solving interesting problems with great teams. There is a headiness to it, like flying on a large plane. You feel it struggling against gravity at takeoff and working hard to remain aloft at cruising altitude. But the dominant experience is of powerful momentum, strength in turbulence, and an inspiring view. A great team goes fast and far with a heavy load.

I think especially warmly of the young team of seven I managed in my last job. We were all well suited for our roles and charged with marketing the division's most profitable product line—two undeniably important factors in the strong results we achieved. But we also enjoyed an extraordinary chemistry that increased what we could deliver for the business. We taught and encouraged each other and spoke candidly about what didn't work. We let our personalities show, bantering and teasing throughout long, intense days at the office. We took interest in each other's hobbies; explored our multiethnic, multinational, and religiously diverse backgrounds, mainly through food; and celebrated birthdays, marriages, and babies—the milestones of mainstream twenty- and thirtysomething lives. We respected and cared about each other.

This is not to say I was their friend. I wasn't. In addition to leading strategy development, my job had been to navigate our team through the ever-changing commercial landscape:

to coach and advocate for them, remove barriers to their success, and protect them from depressing political machinations at higher levels. I didn't burden them with my own work problems and insecurities, or reveal any but the most family-friendly details of my personal life, which would have been unprofessional and unfair. Rather, I prided myself in keeping these, and many other aspects of my self and life, tightly under wraps—perversely so, in retrospect. The fact that I always stayed two glasses of wine behind the team at our social outings didn't escape their notice or cheeky comment.

But I suspect we all knew our professional relationship would graduate to the personal once I was no longer their boss. And indeed, as soon as my old team learned of my accident through the company grapevine (always fast, usually true), they descended on my apartment to greet a thinner, paler, quieter, more tired and uncertain me than they had ever known. There, over pizza and a couple of hours, all the chemistry and caring that had made us so effective at work lifted my spirits tremendously, and I glimpsed a bridge between the isolated land of infirmity I occupied and the world I was working hard to return to.

You can't engineer that kind of chemistry, but you can create the conditions that might spark and sustain it, starting by putting the right people in the right jobs. So, I spend a lot of time preparing interview questions for the final candidates for my new team—a couple of softballs about their prior experience to break the ice, but mainly chewy ones about situations they'd actually face in the job. That way they can show what they'd bring to it, whether or not that's obvious from their résumé.

After two days of preparation, phone interviews, and soliciting feedback on the candidates from their current managers and my colleagues, I make my decision. I extend the offers and am delighted when they are immediately accepted. The winning candidates are talented, experienced, hardworking, and kind. I see mojo in our future. With a bit of direction from me and my gracious colleagues, they can start their jobs without me being in the office, and our new little venture will be that much closer to takeoff when I return. I feel relief and a surge of confidence that I've still got "it." People choose the boss, not just the job, after all—especially when moving within our company, where everyone knows everything about everyone, or can find it out, and the strongest performers are spoiled for choice.

The next day, I'm a hot mess. The hiring process consumed so much energy and attention that I forgot to take all my naps and most of my meals. I am suffering mightily for the self-neglect, and all the tasks on my list for the day feel urgent, yet impossible. I try to review some work strategy papers but can't hold their story line in my head. I need to call my health insurance company to find out why they rejected my latest OT claim but don't feel lucid enough either to comprehend or fight their rationale. My kitchen is devoid of food I can easily prepare, and I can't fathom how I will replenish it.

I feel one of my weekly weeps coming on—the short, mindless crying fits that help me blow off pent-up frustration and sadness—but soon find myself trapped in an epic sobbing and rumination loop instead. I cry because I am exhausted and hungry; because I have been shattered by a couple of light days' work, though I used to have formidable stamina; and because I have caused this setback and let myself down.

Five minutes elapse, then ten, then fifteen. My head and stomach ache, and my hand burns, as always. I pace around my apartment, blowing my streaming nose in wads of toilet paper and taking slow, ragged breaths, but I can't calm myself. I know the storm will eventually pass on its own but that the longer it lasts, the more demoralized I will feel, and the harder it will be to keep slogging away with the self-care. I need to call someone to pull me out of this loop, now.

Over years of solo living I've developed the ability to assess my remote support options almost automatically. Feeling some lack, I'll think, *What is it that I need—encouragement or someone to share in my happiness? Problem-solving or a nonjudgmental ear? Who in my inner circle does that well? Can they bear what I need to unload, without becoming worried or overwhelmed themselves? Will they have time to help?* I also consider how much I have recently asked of the person, as I want to spread my need as thinly as possible. And then, there are very few people I will allow to witness a proper meltdown.

Now I flip open my Motorola Razr and scroll through the lime-green LED names on the tiny black screen until I reach

Dad. Despite his precipitous mood swings, he remarkably never loses his shit when I need to lose mine. He's a retired corporate soldier, so will understand my work concerns. And he is good at dispelling the fear and shame that often cling to the stickiest problems, complicating their resolution. Fifteen years earlier, I had worried how he would receive the news that I'd been laid off from my very first job out of college. "Ha! Congratulations, kid," he'd said with a laugh. "You are now no longer the only working Fogg who *hasn't* been laid off or fired. Don't worry, it'll only happen two or three more times in your life." (He was right about that.) And then he helped me tailor my embryonic résumé to improve my chances of landing interviews.

I haltingly describe the day that is defeating me. "I'm so sorry, kid," Dad says. "But you'll land on your feet. You always do." And he always says that, and I always think, *Maybe I will, maybe I won't,* because nobody always lands on their feet. At least, not with the kind of sturdy, gymnastics-champion plant the expression brings to my mind. But maybe that's not what he means by "land." In any case, his positive outlook on my future helps when my own is hazy or bleak. Then he shifts into management consultant mode. "What are the three things you absolutely have to do, every day, to get better? Can't be any more than three." He speaks to the colleague in me, the determined, kindred spirit with solutions to offer. I find her and bring her forth, gently nudging Her Hot Mess-ness aside.

On Dad's suggestion, I tape signs throughout my apartment:

Live to fight another day and *(1) Eat, (2) Sleep, (3) Hand exercises.* They're crude but effective reminders of what I must do to support tissue healing and nerve regrowth, or else I will struggle to perform the most basic tasks for the rest of my life. Complying means no more work while on medical leave, and ensuring I have time and energy for self-care once back on the job. And that means asking for help when the job demands more than I have to give. This is not my strong suit, as I learned early in my tenure managing that great team, just a couple of years ago.

The role was substantially bigger and more complex than my prior one, and transitioning into it, I'd become uncharacteristically overwhelmed in a way that made the team's jobs harder. And, to my lasting chagrin, I failed to hide my frustration at what I perceived as my boss's lack of support while I struggled. Weeks of building tension peaked in my midyear review, when she articulated my missteps with calm and painful candor. My fitness for the job wasn't at issue, it was my approach to learning it. "Maybe we should have prepared you better," she said, "but you really need to learn how to ask for help."

I wanted to act on her feedback but didn't know where to start. So I asked for, and was granted, an executive coach to help. The coaching process was excruciating, involving data from a battery of personality and leadership tests, and heaps of anonymous feedback from all my closest work contacts. The admiration and goodwill they expressed quickly slipped my mind, while their critiques weighed heavy and long, and for weeks when I awoke each morning, knots in my stomach announced that I was living in unhappy times, before I could remember exactly why.

Like psychotherapy, the coaching process exposed the many disadvantages of my Stoic-leaning worldview, and offered alternatives to it, both gentler and more realistic. I completed it with a more visceral understanding that my achievements weren't the measure of my worth, that nobody accomplishes anything important on their own, and that (as Jen has been trying to drill into my head since I was seventeen) most people like to help. Why not give them the chance, then? With my team and boss's support, I worked hard to put these insights into practice, and they paid off richly in strong business results and high team morale.

Recognizing parallels between that formative experience and the challenges I might face in following Dad's advice, I realize I can again enlist Geri, the woman who coached me before. She responds immediately to my email, and in a subsequent ninety-minute phone conversation we hammer out tactics for handling the scenarios I'm most concerned about, my return-to-work plan chief among them.

Though my boss, Bill, didn't ask for a return date in our brief conversation after the accident, I'd gotten antsy without one myself and later promised him I'd be back in six weeks. With my recovery rate impossible to predict and Dr. Vargas politely unwilling to guess it, I'd seized on six weeks as an outlandishly long medical leave that would surely suffice. Now that my body has vociferously rejected that plan, however, I have no better idea how to define a new, more accurate one. Fortunately, Geri does. "You can't go back to work until you have at least four extra hours of energy at the end of every day," she says firmly. "And the conversation with your boss is not 'Sorry I can't return until . . . '; it's 'I'm psyched to get back, I'll let you know as soon as I'm able, and here's what I'll need when I do.'" It's a simple script, but I need it.

I decide that the conversation with my boss should be in person, like a breakup. So I make an appointment, dig some business casual out of my closet to wear, and catch a 2 train toward downtown Manhattan. I exit at Park Place, then head west along the northern border of Ground Zero, the former site of the World Trade Center.

It is a massive building site today, loud and teeming with hopeful activity like the pages of a Richard Scarry children's book. But whenever I look at it, I see the view from our office windows that tormented my colleagues and me when we returned to our building six months after the attacks: workers in high-visibility jackets, methodically raking through the wreckage-cleared dirt, searching for the last and smallest of human remains, leaving patterns like those in a Japanese rock garden. Whenever they found any, a siren signaled the discovery, and everyone on the site stood at attention while workers somberly walked the remains up the long ramp leading from the deep site foundations to the street. Watching from the office, we stood still, too.

I push through the revolving doors at our front entrance, walk through the main lobby past the memorial to employees killed in 9/11, ascend the escalator to the elevator lobby, and catch one to the forty-first floor. I've made some version of this trek thousands of times, but now I take it in with an outsider's eyes. I also keep my head down and stick to the periphery. I know loads of people here, and as much as I would like to see some friendly faces, I don't have the time or energy to keep repeating my story.

When I knock lightly on the doorframe of Bill's office, he glances back at me from his computer against the wall, smiles warmly, and swivels around to his desk, gesturing for me to take one of the chairs opposite it. I've been apprehensive about our conversation, but my decision doesn't surprise Bill, and he requires no explanation. "Many things in life are complicated, but this one is crystal clear," he says in a soft European accent I have yet to place. "You have only one job to do, and that is to regain your health. Please do not think about anything else." Though I've heard words to the same effect from many people, I feel a heavy emotional weight fall away when I hear them from him.

We spend the rest of our thirty minutes together talking about my accident, surgical repair, and recovery process. He appears so interested in the details—unlike many people, whose eyes start darting around at the word *blood*—that I ask if he wants to see my wound. "Ugh, *God* no!" he blurts out, pulling a face like a little boy gagging on brussels sprouts. This cracks me up because Bill never puts a word or hair out of place. And for the regulars at Bellevue, a glimpse of my wound is as tantalizing as artisanal chocolate. On my way out, I stop for a brief chat with a good friend who sits in the office next to Bill's. She tells me later that he popped his head in after I left. "She's different, isn't she," he'd said.

Released from my unreasonable demands for myself, I am giddy with relief, and my optimism grows, even in my dreams. One takes place in Paris, a favorite city since my sister and I first visited it in college. I arrive at the hotel I have booked as the sun sets, casting the grand, pale building in gold. The hotel clerk unapologetically informs me that no reservation exists in my name, and the property is fully booked—as are all the decent hotels in the city, due to some global industry conference taking place there that week.

"But I have a confirmation email!" I say, waving a crumpled paper in the air between us. He shrugs with his face. "Please, you have to do *something* for me." I am a single woman. Night is falling. I can't go wandering around, alone in the dark, looking for the last available room in Paris.

"Well," he sighs, "there is one place I can put you for the night, but it's not a real room and you absolutely must leave in the morning."

"That's fine. *Anything* is fine. Thank you so much!"

He leads me through a maze of corridors, opens a door, and gestures for me to go in. It is an ancient dungeon, complete with scuttling rats, rusty wrist irons draping fat stone walls, and little heaps of flea-infested hay scattered around the damp

floor, where I am presumably to lay my head. I stare in aston-
ishment and disgust. *Just one night*, I think. *I can do it for one
night.* I begin rolling my suitcase in, then stop. No. *No.* I do
not have to accept this. I can find something else, something
safe, and better than this.

In my waking hours, I'm mostly able to hang on to that
confidence, but it takes consistent effort. I follow the marching
orders I've posted throughout the apartment: *Eat, Sleep, Hand
exercises.* I call loved ones. I try to spot anxious thoughts wea-
seling into my mind and challenge them before they birth
gloomy stories about my future. I know when to boot myself
outdoors for a bit of fresh air and Brooklyn buzz. And as with
life in more normal times, some days are just better than
others.

In OT, Beth has me working to flatten out my hand, which she
estimates will take about three weeks. She doesn't revise the
estimate when I tell her Dr. Vargas already started the process
in my last clinic appointment; she just raises one eyebrow,
Spock-like.

Splint off, right forearm resting palm upward on the OT
table, I place the heel of my left hand against the vertical fingers of my right hand, close my left fingers over the right fingers, and give a nudge. The fingers don't budge. I try a bit
harder, to no avail. I start pushing in earnest, with the kind of
force I would use to shove a box of books, and feel an intense,

mechanical pain in my inner right forearm. I continue nonetheless and move them about a quarter inch. How had Dr.
Vargas been able to move them more? And once I get them
flat, my hand will still be useless, because the fingers don't
move individually and I can't feel anything. Fuck.

Beth stops by, touching the fingertips of one hand to the
table, tucking a sharpened pencil behind her numerously
pierced ear with the other. "How're you doing?"

I know she's talking about the hand flattening, but the question brings to mind my meltdown and the necessity of postpon-
ing my return to work. I look at her, eyes welling as I consider
how much to say in response. She sits down beside me.

"Tough week?" she asks quietly, so that the other patients at
our table would have to strain to hear.

"Yeah."

"We have a great psych department here. I could get you a
referral, if you feel like talking to someone?"

"Nah, that's OK, I already have one, actually. And it does
help . . . I'm just . . . tired."

Beth nods slowly for a moment, eyes trained on mine and
squinting slightly. "Be right back," she says, pushing off the
table and out of her seat. She strides to the unoccupied receptionist's desk and purposefully sifts through the administrative
flotsam collected there, rejected by the clinical storage else-
where in the room. "Do *not* try this at home," she says, back at
our table, sliding a fat rubber-grip pen and scrap of brown
paper across the table to me. "Sign your name."

She sits down, elbows on the table, chin on clasped hands, watching me. I look at her, eyebrows raised. Until now she has sternly forbidden active motion with my right hand.

"Go ahead." She smiles. "It'll be OK as long as you go slow and gentle. And *only* do it here. With me."

Picking up a pen. Such a simple, fluid action in normal circumstances. Automatic. I think, *I should jot that down*, but I don't have to think about how I'll do it. I only have to shape the idea I want to capture, while my brain works in the background, translating my intentions into commands for the hand so that it follows along. But these days I have the dexterity of a garden rake, and lacking a lifetime of experience with it, my brain has not automated the process of manipulating the clunky tool. So I must consciously break the action of picking up a pen into tiny segments, like different frames of a stop-motion Claymation movie, and try to execute them as fluidly as possible.

I use my stiff fingers to hook the pen, drag it toward me, and orient the tip to four o'clock. I press my thumb and forefinger into it lightly and flip my hand palm upward. I tuck my middle finger under the pen, tipping its point up so that its weight rests on the bottom joint of my index finger, and I can scooch the tripod of my thumb, index, and middle fingers closer to the point. I rest the pinky side of my hand on the table, grip the pen a little tighter, place the point on the paper, and very slowly begin to guide it in the cursive loops, lashes, and switchbacks of my name. Because I can't feel the pen, I watch the product of its every movement to check that my hand is doing what I mean it to.

And there she is: *Rebecca D. Fogg*.

My normal signature is a flourishy mess, reflecting the speed and thoughtlessness with which I usually execute it, and perhaps a touch of bravado and passive aggression as well. *I will follow all your rules, Taxman*, it says, *but* on this form *I will cross the lines!* The signature I have executed at Beth's instruction, however, is contained, angular, and tentative, the inky lines alternately heavy and light because I cannot apply constant pressure while making the many micro-adjustments necessary to guide the point.

Still, it is easily recognizable as mine, and I feel a visceral sense of reunion with my self. My new hand *works*. It works, and it proves that some part of the connection between my mind and my hand has not been lost, because the shapes it produces are those it has always produced, ever since I was eight and my sister taught me to write my name in cursive on our playroom chalkboard. There will be no more active exercises for several weeks yet, but Beth has made her point. I am healing, and life won't always feel so difficult and unpredictable.

I flatten my hand in four days instead of Beth's predicted three weeks, and after easily overlooked progress measured in millimeters and decimal points by professional instruments, progress that I can see for myself accelerates. Beth releases me from my splint at home during the day, and enjoying the freedom to use my naked hand, albeit gently, I feel like a teen-ager acting recklessly with permission.

From hand flattening, I graduate to mobilizing one finger joint at a time. The exercises are tedious: Press left fingers down on the right index finger, just below the top joint, to isolate it. Now try to move that joint, and watch it do almost nothing, for days, until you've finally broken through some invisible wall and your effort results in the desired movement. Repeat the exercise with the top joints of middle, ring, and little fingers, and the thumb; then the middle joint of the index finger, and so on; bottom joint of index finger, and so on.

Mobile joints enable me to tackle composite movements— bending fingers toward palm, touching thumb to each finger pad, forming fists and hooks. Then fondling fist-sized pom-poms (because that's all you're doing, until you can finally close your digits enough to pick it up), then crumpling nap-kins on the table, then finally, picking up a cup and managing not to drop it. When I can build a whole stack of cups, I smile to myself thinking of the patient with the pin-tipped fingers, who had assured me on my very first day of OT that I would reach this milestone.

When Beth introduces strength exercises, I am right back at square one, this time feebly pressing putty into the therapy table, then lightly gripping it, then squeezing putties offer-ing increasing levels of resistance and, at last, pushing my re-paired tendons to their new limits with a spring-resistance gripper tool.

The final phase of the OT plan, an eclectic range of dexterity exercises, leverages all that I have gained—strength, a wide range of motion, and small, coordinated motor movements. I pinch clothespins on and off a line, dig coins out of putty and pick them up off the floor, grasp skinny pegs and place them into a pegboard while Beth times me. Sweet Jesus, I hate that last one, watching the single hand on Beth's stopwatch spin round as I chase escaping pegs across the table, accidentally flicking them off it instead of sticking them into their holes, then standing up to chase them across the floor. It's galling. Performing virtually the same task with Lite-Brite pegs (Google it) as a five-year-old, my only difficulty had been keeping my family's pet guinea pig, who often escaped his cage, from eating them.

The issue is my complete lack of sensation. Of the five digits on my right hand, only the little finger and the side of my ring finger closest to it still have sensation, because the nerve that serves them was not severed in the accident. Except when they hurt, the rest of the digits are silent, like a dead radio, receiving and transmitting nothing about the outside world. As a result, my dexterity is abysmal—as if I am always working with winter gloves on.

The lack of sensation doesn't worry me yet, though. While the Tinel sign—the tap-elicited tingling along the regenerating nerve—suggests the latter has only grown a few centimeters beyond the wound site, it is making good progress, and must reach its targets deep in my hand before I will experience its full benefit, whatever that may be. And by many other mea-sures, I am healing well. The once-angry wound has settled down to a thin, pink seam, the sickly bruise that stained my inner forearm has disappeared, and with the swelling all but gone, my hand looks nearly as it did before the accident. My pain has diminished to the point that I only need hydroco-done at night; less burdened by pain and medication, I have much more energy and no longer require a daily nap.

Now I don't just plod back and forth between home, Belle-vue's surgery outpatient clinic, and its Upper Extremity Oc-cupational Therapy Room, the three planets in my trauma universe; I can engage in the world beyond them. After OT ap-pointments, I sneak into the medical library on the hospital campus or go to the nearby medical bookstore and surrepti-tiously unwrap surgery texts, in search of keys for decoding Dr. Vargas's report on my operation. Luxuriating in early April's un-seasonable warmth and sunshine, I trade smiles with strangers during my daily walks and linger on the promenade or in Brook-lyn Bridge Park afterward to do hand exercises; make right-handed journal entries; and call Jen, my sister, or my parents to report on my progress and what I have learned about the science behind it. Selecting music on my iPod, the dial clicks right past Bach and lands on Prince, seemingly of its own accord.

This period brings a subtle shift in my experience of Bellevue, too. Though still a patient, I now possess knowledge and confidence enough to contribute to the community that has given me so much. In clinic, I can quickly recap the salient details of my case for residents rotating onto my team who haven't had a chance to read my entire medical record. In OT, I can encourage new patients the way other patients did me when I first arrived. I am careful not to tell them everything will be OK, because if there's anything we in the Bellevue Upper Extremity Occupational Therapy Room know, it's that life is dangerous and uncertain. But I can greet them, witness their efforts, and cheer their successes.

As for my own rehabilitation, Beth has started saying, "That should make you feel more confident about returning to work," whenever I achieve a new milestone. And one day in mid-May, when a stranger in the Bellevue elevator tells me they've seen me coming and going for weeks and that I look like I have "turned a corner," I know Beth is right. It's time to plan my return to work, though the thought still makes me uneasy.

That weekend, I slowly wake up at my dining table with peanut-buttered wheat toast and a big mug of espresso with hot milk. Eyes on the novel that I hold open with my left hand, I pick up my mug with my right and take a sip of the brew, an affordable luxury I buy from a century-old Greenwich Village roaster. I let it pool in my mouth for a moment, as I often do to savor its strong, smooth flavor, before swallowing and re-placing the mug on the table so that I can turn another page. This time, however, I pause after swallowing, and immediately take another sip. There is something different about the ritual today. I concentrate on the taste of the coffee. No, not that. Then what? Scanning my consciousness, I know the difference is sensory but, strangely, not what it is. And then I do. Today, for the first time in about a hundred days, I can feel the warmth of the coffee cup in my right hand.

It's not warmth the way I used to feel it; it's some new sensation, but still warmth, and I'm elated. It means that some of the temperature-registering axons in my median nerve have successfully sprouted growth cones and crept all the way from my wrist through my hand to reach their targets. And that means that axons in other types of neurons—those that trigger sensations of pain and vibrations and tell me the position of my hand in space—might, too. Here is the best sign yet that I will regain enough sensation to keep my hand safe, and to do the precise and delicate work that my independence depends upon.

I jump out of my chair and go to the kitchen to run my hand under hot water. Yup, that's warm, too. I turn on the cold water—cold sensation is back, too! I open up the freezer and squeeze a bag of frozen peas. Ouch! Burning, burning cold. I'm astonished by these developments, and sentimentally imagine that this must be what it's like to feel a baby's first in utero movements. (Later, my unsentimental mom friends correct me. Baby's first movements just feel like gas, apparently.) I'd just told my boss I'd return to work the following week. Finally, I feel ready to go.

16
....

Struggling with the
Status Quo

Late May 2006. The brisk clicking of my high heels on lino-
leum broadcasts my first visit to Bellevue as a full-time business professional, rather than full-time patient, and I have
worn a super-smart pantsuit to mark the occasion. I've come
for a checkup with Dr. Vargas, who has finished his term as
chief resident of the hand-surgery team but is standing in for
his successor this week.

He has been a regular presence in my mind since my
last appointment with him in February. Because of the sensitivity he has shown through our interactions, I have imagined him appreciating my challenges and efforts to a degree
that my loved ones cannot always achieve. As I make my
way to the hospital's outpatient clinic, I look forward to
showing off my progress, and hope he will find it heartening,
too.

The nurse shows me to an exam room that's larger than

others I've seen, furnished with a periwinkle-blue papered ex-amination table on one side, built-in desk occupied by a large computer on the other, and two shelves above it supporting a smattering of medical texts. The paper sheet crackles and rips as I seat myself on the exam table, cross my legs, and pull my BlackBerry out of my pocket to scan emails.

I hear footfalls at the door not long after I've settled in, and look up to see Dr. Vargas standing in front of me, smiling broadly. Grinning back, I raise my right hand and flutter my fingers; he flips his palms up in response, as if to say, *Look at you!* I don't know if this is his invitation to do so, but I hop off the table and we hug: a rich exchange of sentiment, free of language's constraints. Then I hop back up onto the exam table and hold out my right forearm, scar side up.

"How's the pain?" he asks, lightly taking my wrist in his hands, thumbs atop and fingers beneath it, tilting it left and right so he can see how the wound has healed.

"Good. I mean, minimal," I respond, watching his hands on my wrist, wondering how it looks through his eyes. "I'm totally off the drugs now."

"Great. What about sensation?" Now he's holding my wrist in one hand, tapping with the index finger of the other along the path of the median nerve. He doesn't have to tell me that he's checking for the Tinel sign and wants me to tell him where I stop feeling the little sparks that indicate recent tissue reinnervation.

"There," I say when he has just crossed the heel of my hand.

The nerve has grown a little over three inches in about four months, a healthy pace. "*And* I can feel hot and cold now. But nothing else."

"That's still good progress. All the sensations don't return at once." He needs to perform a few more sensory tests for the record nonetheless, so he pulls a tweezer-like tool out of his pocket, and I close my eyes. Lightly supporting my open hand at the wrist, he pokes my palm in different spots with the tool, sometimes with one prong, sometimes with two, to see whether I can distinguish between the sensations. I can't, which is not surprising. Two-point discrimination is a sophisticated sensory task, which regenerated peripheral nerves rarely perform.

My ability to feel light touch is also severely compromised. In OT, Beth tests this by touching, then stroking, my palm with paintbrush-like tools that have varying numbers of stiff bristles. But because surgeons don't have these tools in the outpatient hand clinic, Dr. Vargas uses a capped pen. I sometimes feel a slight trail of pressure and vibration when he draws it across different parts of my palm, but almost nothing when he touches it lightly in various spots. I can, however, perceive the difference between sharp and dull pain, which Dr. Vargas proves to us both by alternately pressing the capped pen and one prong of the tweezer thing into my palm. Not something I'd tried at home.

The sensory tests completed, Dr. Vargas next asks me to perform a round of my current OT exercises. Despite having read Beth's notes about my progress since our last appointment, when I couldn't even open my hand, he's nodding and "wow"ing as I run through my repertoire of hooks, fists, and fans.

"What about dexterity?" he asks.

"Lousy. Buttons, keys, fiddly things like that, are a nightmare. But I can type! And that's what my hands spend most of their time doing, so . . ." I shrug.

"You can *type*? But you have to look at the keys because you can't feel where your fingers should go, right?" he asks, looking up at me.

"No! I make tons of mistakes, but I'm fast. I can correct them as soon as I see them on-screen."

"Amazing," he says, now holding up two fingers in front of me, a near Boy Scout salute. I squeeze them hard to demonstrate my grip strength, eliciting a slight wince. All this exertion makes my hand hurt, and I cradle it in my left elbow to give it a rest.

A clinic checkup would normally end at this point, but Dr. Vargas continues. "Amazing," he says again, eyes on my hand, then at me. "You've far exceeded our expectations. You're a really good healer."

"What did you expect?"

He pauses, then says, "We were all really worried about you . . . Dr. Matthews, Dr. Espinoza, the attending in charge of the department . . . everyone is very happy for you now."

A nurse taps on the doorframe, and Dr. Vargas steps out of the room for a second. I can't hear their words, but when he reenters, he takes a seat in one of the two rolling office chairs, and I know he's bought us a little time for my inevitable questions. I pull a list out of my workbag, along with a copy of his operative report, which I've underlined as profusely as I did my college English Lit reading. I've also sketched the cross-section of a peripheral nerve in the margins of the report and annotated it with more questions.

Dr. Vargas doesn't stay seated for long. After my first couple of questions, he's leaning over my diagram to point out the landmarks associated with his explanations, then pulling an anatomy book off the shelf to find other instructive visuals, and animating his descriptions with gestures when all else fails. "Ah. *That's* a good one. The *reason* you don't know where your hand is when you wake up in the morning, until you open your eyes to look for it," he explains, now holding his right arm high in the air, "is *proprioception.*" Now eyes closed and touching his right palm with his left index finger. "It's another kind of sensory experience that your peripheral nerves mediate, telling you where your body is in space."

Often, he doesn't just answer the question I ask; he anticipates my one or two follow-up questions, and answers those. Scribbling notes as fast as he can speak, which is New York fast, I am in nerd heaven. Finally, I cross the last question off my list, and reluctantly start packing up my notes. We both know it's high time to clear out.

"All right, then," Dr. Vargas says, picking his clipboard up off the counter opposite the exam table, "we don't need to see you again for six months, for your surgical sign-off appointment." By "we," Dr. Vargas means whoever is running the hand team at that point, which won't be him.

"Ah, OK. Well, that's good news, I guess."

"But if the pain gets worse, or sensation isn't coming back, you may want to see a specialist," he says as he fills out the slip of paper I'll need to give to the clinic clerk to make the sign-off appointment.

"Could that be you?"

"I'm about to start a fellowship in a different specialty, and you'll need someone board-certified in Hand. So I can't treat you anymore," he says, looking up to hand me the slip. "But you can leave a message for me, or any of the guys, in the plastics department here if you need a referral." Then, after a second, "Or just to tell us how you are doing. It's nice to get good news."

"I will definitely do that," I respond. But assuming this is our last-ever meeting, I tell him again how much the care I've received at Bellevue, and particularly from him, has meant to me.

"Well, you've been phenomenal through all this," he says, smiling. No rush, no awkwardness, unlike our first follow-up appointment. "You're a real survivor." I give him a last, quick hug, then we walk into the hallway, and he sees me off with a nod as I hurry to a 10:00 a.m. meeting.

En route to the office, my chest feels hot and tight, as it has every day since my return a couple of weeks prior. My body won't let me forget my former boss's words, even when I'm not thinking them: "It takes six months to learn a job, but you've got to prove yourself in three." I remind myself to take slow, deep breaths, and listen to "Razor" by the Foo Fighters on repeat through the whole commute, every single day. With lyrics about "cutting away" and saying goodbye, fans suspect the song is about suicide, though the band has never confirmed it. In any case, it's not the lyrics that soothe me. It's the singer's quiet but resolved voice, the tender melody and the dissonance of its refrain against the undulating acoustic guitar backdrop. Reflecting my inner weather, these elements loosen the molten knots in my body.

Arriving at work, the unconstrained warmth of colleagues, many of whom I consider friends, calms and buoys me. Like the moms who visit with their new babies during maternity leave, I can hardly walk down the hall without getting stopped by someone who wants to ask after my health. They express gratitude for my recovery and ask if it would be too painful to tell them "what really happened," because some of the rumors are even wilder than reality. Moved by the fear and sadness I often see in their eyes as we talk, I rush to reassure them that everything is OK now. But when one friend says, with mischievous delight, "I heard your whole arm was dangling by a thread!" I regale him with the gory details he craves.

I find it fitting that the first job of my second life is about finding new opportunities. What do our target customers want or need that we don't yet deliver? Do we have, or could we acquire, the assets and capabilities to deliver it? If so, would the financial return merit the investment? As I settle in, I enjoy pursuing the answers with my colleagues, especially when it entails exploring external partnerships.

A meeting toward that end with one company is unremarkable, except that I get a good vibe from their analytics guy. He's the most junior of them—and probably years younger than I am—but he knows his stuff, and he lets fly a few quips during his presentation that make everyone laugh despite a dry subject. Our eyes meet at one point, and he smiles. I like his eyes and the look of his forearms in rolled-up shirtsleeves.

My colleagues and I don't meet with the company again. But they're clearly pitching to other parts of our business, because I run into Analytics Guy at work several times over the next few weeks, and when he invites me to lunch, I assume it's a networking thing. I realize it's not when, after trading professional summaries, he tells me he's seriously thinking of a career change, which you absolutely do not tell someone you hope can assist with your current gig. That little existential bread crumb leads to bigger and bigger ones, until we are engaged in full-on, fantastic brain sex.

I love brain sex, even more than sex sex, which I like quite a lot. The thrill of new knowledge, the tingle of a daring hypothesis, the playfulness of brainstorming or debate . . . it's an orgy of mental marvelousness that I never take for granted. It doesn't depend on affection or physical attraction; you can have it with anyone, whatever your genre of relationship. But combined with these, it's the dating lottery jackpot. So I'm pleased when Analytics Guy texts me the next day to make a date for the weekend. We begin "seeing each other," which in NYC dating lingo falls on the more committed end of the continuum between a fling and a relationship.

As summer ripens, the patterns of my accident and recovery become clearer, consolidating into a picture of astonishing good fortune. So many people rallied to my aid. So many people told me they loved me, out loud and often. My care team was as ambitious for my recovery as I was. I'd had the opportunity to dedicate myself entirely to recovery and am getting more able with my "new" hand every day. And the pain and suffering I'd endured have become a mere fact that I recollect, rather than an embodied experience I can't shake off.

Soon I'm tripping on full-blown survivor's euphoria. Everything is perfect as it is, yet all good things are possible. It's OK if I never get another promotion! But when my boss presses me to define my ultimate career goal at the company, I blurt out "general manager," though I'd never aspired to the job before. It's OK if I never marry! But Analytics Guy and I are having a ball together, and I think, *Surely this is how all lasting relationships begin.* It's OK if I end up with poor sensation in my replanted hand! But I've been lucky in recovery so far . . . I bet I'll be lucky in axon regeneration, too. I virtually dance through my days like an urban reboot of Disney's Snow White, perpetually surrounded by chirping birds because wherever I go, and whatever I do, there's something worth singing about.

By early autumn, after forty-five Bellevue appointments and over three hundred hours of OT, the new instrument on the end of my right arm is *my* instrument. Beth gives me the briefest of hugs at our last appointment and shoos me away before I can finish my heartfelt thank-you speech. "Aaaaah, get outta here! All my patients are so sentimental. But you guys don't belong here."

In late autumn, my euphoria deflates with the rude sound of a punctured balloon when Analytics Guy and I call it quits, after an unpleasant handful of weeks of slowing calls and failing to talk about what we've independently concluded: We're both trying to figure out what we want out of life next, and with too few common certainties between us, chemistry alone can't hold us together. I'm irrationally angry at him—not for his rejection, since I can't imagine a future with him, either, but for his unwitting injury to the sense of gratitude and possibility I've determinedly wrung from my traumatic experience. I'm afraid of losing it forever, and realize that if I want it to persist, I will have to work hard to sustain it.

My first thought is to volunteer at Bellevue, where I've found emotional nourishment throughout recovery and might help others do the same. After jumping through a bunch of administrative hoops, I am cleared to join the hospital's long-standing patient-visiting program and assigned to the trauma surgical recovery ward where I had spent the night following my surgery.

Each Saturday morning, the week's accumulated tension

falls off my body like hunks of melting glacier as I make my way through the hospital's identification checkpoints and corridors to the ward. Stopping by the nurse's station, I jot down the names and room numbers of patients occupying the ward that week on a small notepad, then I visit each room. I am (rightfully) not allowed access to information about the reasons for their stays, but I know that all will have undergone some type of major reconstructive surgery, whether precipitated by a traumatic accident, or disease interventions like amputation of a limb due to diabetes or removal of a malignant tumor.

Through awkward trial and error, I've learned that nobody wants to admit they are so bored, lonely, or scared that they need companionship from a total stranger, and that the more confident I appear in my purpose, the more readily they will open up, if that's what they want to do. So I walk into each room like I own it, look the patient in the eye, smile brightly, and say, "Hi! My name is Becca. I'm a volunteer here, and my *whole job* is just to talk with people!" Then I shut up and stare, still smiling, until the patient responds—an annoying but effective tactic my psychiatrist uses on me all the time. People who don't want to talk glance briefly at me, then away, and murmur, "Uh, no. Thanks," and I move on. Those who do want to talk return my gaze and start asking questions.

"You . . . just talk to people?" is a common opener.

"Yup, that's it."

"*Why?*" (Meaning, "You are crazy to come here *on purpose.*")

"I used to be a patient here."

"You *were*? What happened to you?"

I tell my story, then listen carefully to figure out where the patient wants to go from there. If I sense that they want to keep talking but not about themselves, I look for clues about their interests—maybe a book, a framed photo, or some kind of audio player on their bedside table—and ask questions about them. If all else fails, food is a great icebreaker. I ask, "What do you want to eat first when you get out of here?" and watch people's tired eyes light up as they describe mouthwatering recipes from myriad cultures and implant their memories of meaningful meals in my mind.

My marital status is also of near-universal interest, unfortunately, and I am repeatedly stymied by the question "What're you waiting for?" because not only is it one I have no desire to answer, but also, responses to deeply personal questions can expose differences—in values and beliefs—that might hinder connection or agitate rather than soothe. And I'm here to soothe, if I can.

I'm better at gracefully receiving the patients' well-intended wishes ("Dear Lord, please reward your faithful servant Rebecca with a *good man!*") and compliments ("You're friendly. You've got a great story. If only you had a dog, you'd be the *whole package!*").

Many patients respond to my story of injury with their own.

I can usually bear it easily, inspired by the dignity and fortitude with which they bear their circumstances. And given my newfound passion for medical science, I am always intrigued. However, a small number patients them have endured such gruesome injuries or repairs that I have to freeze my face and body to keep from betraying an inner recoiling upon first sight of their unhealed wounds; and the stories accompanying them are inevitably tough.

More often, it's patients' existential distress that puts a catch in my throat. They wonder aloud: *How many more operations can I stand, and will they do any good in the end? Will my young child ever overcome the trauma of witnessing my bloody accident? How much can I teach my teenager about life before this terminal disease kills me? Does God judge me for fearing death?* They know I can't answer those questions; they just need to voice them to someone who cares about what they are feeling and won't be scared off by it. I know this because that's what I needed during my recovery; it's what many people need in hard times. In response, I do what others did for me: I listen closely, ask the occasional question so they know I'm listening, and try to find some non-cliché way to tell them I'm sorry for what they're going through.

I take my leave when the patients stop filling the silences I leave open for them. After the visits that upset me, I lean up against the wall outside their doors to collect myself before moving on to the next room. The hospital staff never intrude on these moments; they know exactly what I'm doing. The patients stay on my mind after every shift, and for months as I fall asleep at night, I silently recite the accumulating names of everyone I've visited. Carol, who asked God to give me a "good man" . . . Pedro, with the 9/11 tattoo . . . Santos, with the BBQ sauce recipe . . . Elaine, who wants me to eat more fruit . . . Mickey, who's nervous about his surgery next week . . . Nick, who goes back to prison soon.

When patients thank me for my visits, I tell them in all honesty that I benefit from them as much as they do. We're obsessed with the same existential questions, like *Who will I be when this is all over?* And they share interesting perspectives I haven't considered. They bring out the best in me, and it feels good to give it. Most of all, I feel that Death Club kinship with them, and calm in the certainty that I am living to the fullest when we are together. This *is what life is about*, I think as I walk back through the long corridors to the exit each week. *Whatever else happens, we have given each other* this.

On December 26, 2006, I celebrate my fortieth birthday with a small party, including Dad and Kate. It's a lovely evening, but what I'm really excited about is the "handiversary" party I've decided to throw on the anniversary of the accident, which falls a few weeks later, on a January Saturday. On the night of the handiversary party, my apartment is filled to capacity with people who helped me through recovery. Guests of honor include Erica, Jen, and their husbands; my Brooklyn posse; and Mom and Charlie, who arrive laden with special-occasion Southern food that Mom has contrived to pack for travel from Nashville—her own thanks offering to my guests. I'd been pleased when Dr. Vargas, now deep into his new specialty training, accepted the invitation I mailed to the hospital for him and guests, and he arrives with a couple of surgery buddies in tow, all visibly enthusiastic in anticipation of a rare night out on the town.

Moving through the party to greet guests and peddle cocktails, I watch the various realms of my life colliding and emitting sparks of pleasure: family meeting neighbors, business school meeting choir, college meeting hospital, finance meeting massage therapy . . . merry clusters dissolving and reforming in different combinations throughout the evening, putting names to faces and discovering the common qualities I value in them. There's always one cluster sitting on the floor around my coffee table, writing in the guest book I've left out, and another standing in front of a large portrait of me painted by Julie, of the Brooklyn posse, who is a very talented artist. "I'm traumatized by your trauma," she'd said a few weeks after my accident. "Can I paint you?" I'd consented, thinking that her creative act might be the only positive outcome of the accident.

The portrait depicts me in profile from the waist up, facing right toward an off-canvas light source. I'm holding my right arm up at the elbow with my left hand, with my newly stitched wound facing the viewer, and the light brightens my face against the darkness of my long hair, clothing, and the teal background. Julie captured the complexity of my feelings in the first weeks of recovery so well that I gasped the first time I saw the painting, nine months later. "She's gotten the shape of your scar exactly right," Dr. Vargas says at the party, tracing his finger in the air across my painted wrist.

After my last guests leave at 4:00 a.m., I stay up another half hour, reading comments left in the guest book and savoring vignettes from the night. Closing the book, I am closing out the year of the accident—and plunging into my second life in earnest.

As 2007 unfolds, I remain keen on my independent science studies and Bellevue volunteering. I also enroll in an evening writing class, where I continue to flesh out the narrative of my accident experience and explore the existential questions it forced me to confront. I love the process of writing, and trading stories and insights with my classmates.

The contrast between these activities and how I spend most of my days is sharp and increasingly problematic. I'd banked on my promotion to VP unlocking new levels of challenge and satisfaction, but it's not panning out that way. The work itself isn't as interesting as I'd expected, and it's not delivering the results my colleagues and I had hoped for. And compared to the crucial work I see patients, nurses, and surgeons doing every week at Bellevue, our purely commercial mandate has lost its power to motivate me. I continue to work hard mainly as a matter of honor and commitment to my colleagues.

As the US plummets into recession between mid-2007 and early 2008, our experimental department gets disbanded, and we are parachuted into other jobs around the division. Then a large reorganization eliminates a number of jobs, including my own, leaving those of us displaced to compete with each other for fewer jobs.

My personal life is up in the air, too. By age thirty-five, the vast majority of my friends had married (twelve with me bridesmaiding them down the aisle), and most had started families. So while our mutual affection persists, our shared life, which was most of my personal life, evaporated in just a few years. It's as though I'd been at a fantastic party, popped to the bathroom for a minute, and come back to an empty room. The surprise exodus makes me all the more grateful that Jen and I have worked hard, and successfully, to remain an active part of each other's lives since she became a married parent, though we naturally see each other much less.

Thus, my mid-thirties had marked the beginning of an accumulating ache of bereavement as old and new friends continued to peel off our once-common path. The conventional salve would have been to get married myself, but I can't force the stars to align in favor of the kind of forever partnership I would want. Or I could have jumped onto the parenting bandwagon. Kids and I generally like each other, probably because I appreciate curiosity and silliness, and I often feel a twinge of envy when I see parents and their teenagers enjoying one another's company. But as my friends contemplated egg freezing, IVF, sperm donors, surrogates, and adoption, I realized that I only wanted to be a mother with a romantic partner. I've never wanted a child "no matter what," and that's the kind of conviction I'd need to contentedly forgo other meaningful paths in order to single-parent well.

The only way forward was to reinvent my personal life. So I worked to deepen casual acquaintances and to meet people through new activities—a choir, a running club, salsa dancing, art classes. Eventually I found a strong sense of community in the choir and my Brooklyn posse, though I knew that the shape and intensity of those friendships would change, too, and probably sooner rather than later. I'd finally grasped a fundamental law of adulting: life, for everyone, is starting over, all the time.

What does that mean for me now—single, just crossed over into middle age, and waiting for the axe to fall on my job? Turning this question over and over in my mind to no avail, I feel bone-weary and untethered. Gradually, however, it reframes itself into one I can answer: Do I want to spend my hard-won second life grasping at the fringes of my friends' family lives, and relentlessly pursuing one of my own that may never materialize, or do I want to find out what it is like to live fully, exactly as I am, right now? That, *that*.

And then another question, thrilling to contemplate, tumbles after it: Given there's no avoiding painful change, and I have no one depending upon me, what could I do with my life that would be impossible if I were on a more traditional path? The seeds of an answer arrive in early 2008, in an email from my company's London office. Subject line: *Interested?*

17

·········

New Normal: My Right
Hand Today

If my hands were shoes, they'd be a pair of sturdy, old brogues. Not elegant, but perfectly presentable when tidied up, and excelling in utility. My long, slender fingers are bisected by knobby knuckles as wrinkled as elephant eyes. My thumbs are not much fatter than my fingers, and the joints of my left thumb are noticeably more mobile than those of my right— due, I suspect, to extensive violin practice at a young age, as the thumb is the hand's moving platform for the instrument, while the other digits perform their gymnastics up and down the strings. I keep my round-bedded nails clipped short so they don't get in the way, another legacy of violin playing, and polish-free because I can't be bothered to maintain it. My cuticles are a mess.

The backs of my hands are veiny, like my mother's, and in recent years slackening skin there has begun to bunch up into fine lines around skeletal landmarks, like elevation bands on a topographical map. I didn't think it possible, but my palms are wrinkly now, too. A few small burn scars advertise my impatience in the kitchen, and in summertime, slow-healing scratches reflect the savage abandon with which I approach rose gardening—a new hobby that landed me in hospital for a night during England's first COVID-19 lockdown, after a giant thorn injected me with some wicked bacteria. I'm considering falconry gauntlets for the next big prune. Not all my hand markings are accidental, though. Almost every day, I ballpoint-pen my top to-dos on the back of my left hand and reapply as necessary after handwashing. It's been a habit since high school, and friends used to ask why I did it. "I'll lose a piece of paper, but I'm not going to lose my hand," I'd say.

I adorn my fingers from a small collection of chunky or sparkly rings, usually one on my right ring finger, occasionally one on my left as well. Sometimes I think twice about the left-hand one, as while I'm not on a mission to find a romantic partner, I am open to the possibility. But oh, horror of horrors! What if I meet some great guy and he thinks I'm married because I'm wearing a ring—*that looks nothing like a wedding or engagement ring*—on that finger? As if a very interested man wouldn't seek to clarify my status, or I couldn't make the first move, as I've done on occasion. I hate how much heteronormative BS I've internalized.

My accident scar is so thin and faint that it usually escapes notice. Once, while straphanging on the New York subway with a crowd of rush-hour commuters, I saw the passenger opposite me eyeing it. Noticing my gaze, he looked at me meaningfully, and I wished I could tell him I was OK, that the scar was not the result of a suicide attempt. The other visual evidence of my accident is also seldom noted. If I make a fist, then bend it down ninety degrees, you'll see skin bunching up around the scar. That's where internal scar tissue has tethered the repaired tendons to my skin, so that when they contract enough, they pull the skin with it. If you watch the underside of the wrist closely while I open and close my hand, you'll see a few small lumps moving together, back and forth beneath the skin. That's the scarring on the repaired tendons themselves.

I am a tactile person. If (global health emergencies allowing) we meet in a professional setting, I'll introduce myself with a smile and a firm handshake, unless local custom dictates otherwise. If you are a friend arriving at my home for a party, I'll take you lightly by the shoulders and draw you in for a kiss on either cheek. If you are an American friend, you'll probably have pulled me into a bear hug before I think to nab you (I have become a bit more physically reserved after over a decade in Britain), but I'll relish it and pat you on the back a couple of times when it's time to part and find you a drink. Then in shared moments of mirth throughout the night, I'll rest my hand on your shoulder, or we'll stand arms around waists for a few seconds, while talking. I suffered mightily for the loss of such contact during the first sixteen months of the COVID-19 pandemic.

I'm not a big gesticulator in conversation, but my hands rarely rest. Even when working, one or the other is usually tensed over my laptop keyboard, or swiping Kindle pages, or gripping a pen in preparation to take notes on something I'm reading. In solitude, and occasionally in the presence of friends, I twirl my hair with my left hand in a precise and intricate pattern. I've done it since toddlerhood, as evidenced by a picture of me at three, standing in a red and navy bathing suit on some beach, with a thumb in my mouth and a hand buried in my bowl cut. I used to twirl with both hands—not at the same time, that would look ridiculous—but no longer, as my right hand's sensory deficits make it *no fun* on that side (more on that below). I don't twirl in response to stress, as my third-grade teacher suggested to my mother, but because it feels really nice.

Watching my right hand in motion, you'd think it typical in every way, and in some ways it nearly is. I've only minor deficits in strength, and my range of motion is excellent, the repaired tendons gliding smoothly and extensively, if not as independently of each other as tendons typically do. This means the fingers don't move as independently, either. But having lived with the impairment for years now, I've concluded it will only pose a problem if I ever need to shoot webs out of my wrist like Spider-Man.

From a sensory perspective, my right hand differs vastly from its pre-accident state along the median nerve distribution. You know that buzzy feeling you get when your foot falls asleep after you've sat too long in an awkward position? That's what most of my right hand feels like, all the time. Numb, but also *like something*. It feels the way white noise sounds, or the way on-screen static at the end of a television broadcasting day used to look.

My perception of external stimuli ranges from poor to intriguingly bizarre. For starters, I have very little light-touch sensibility. One result is that I don't know I'm holding something thin and light in my right hand unless I keep my eyes or mind on it while gripping, which is totally unnatural, so I inevitably drop the object. With an impairment like that, you only have to lose your passport in the airport once before you learn to hold anything important in your more able hand.

Other mishaps due to lack of light touch don't have such an easy fix, like the time I hopped on the London Overground to visit a friend in an unfamiliar part of town. Fearing I'd missed my stop, I wanted to look at a map before I'd gone too far in the wrong direction. The map being inconveniently located above and behind my head, I grasped my left knee with my right hand for leverage, and pulled my torso around from the hips in a good old yoga twist, to get a proper look.

When the young woman sitting to my left jumped in her seat and whipped right to glare at me, I realized I'd grasped her knee, not mine. You'd think I'd have noticed that *my* knee wasn't feeling the grip of my hand, and promptly redirected the errant appendage. But apparently the knee sensation wasn't the "motor mission accomplished" cue my brain was looking for. "Oh my God, I'm so sorry!" I gasped at the woman. "I don't have any sensation in this hand, I swear!" I said, holding it up as if she should have been able to see what I couldn't feel. The look on her face said she categorically rejected my excuse.

While I often don't feel an immobile stimulus contacting my hand, however, I'll register a moving one, like my cat's tail swatting my palm, or a towel as I dry my hands. But I can't discriminate texture; everything feels more or less like sandpaper. Whether a stimulus is moving or not, I'll register its temperature, but I'll perceive it as more extreme than would a typical hand. So a cup of coffee that feels pleasantly hot in my left hand feels unbearably hot in my right, and a cool brass doorknob feels downright cold.

I don't perceive temperature immediately, though, which is dangerous because my skin can be damaged whether I feel a noxious stimulus or not. This quirk is the genesis of my brother-in-law's affectionate nickname for me: Asbestos Hands. "You should be able to flip steaks on the grill without tongs, right?" he said once. Naturally, I accepted the dare, and it turns out that if I'm fast enough, neither human nor bovine flesh burns. Sharp stimuli present a similar difficulty, in that I often don't perceive them until they've broken my skin. For obvious reasons, I'm less cavalier about this issue than delayed temperature perception.

Localization of stimuli on my right hand makes me laugh, when it doesn't make me cuss. That's because I feel whatever is happening to my hand in median nerve territory both at the true locus of a stimulus and in random patches all over my hand. For instance, if I squeeze my first fingertip, it feels as though the top half of my hand is in a vise grip. Poor localization is no problem if a finger gets wet, but it's annoying if a finger gets pricked, and it sucks if a hangnail gets inflamed. That can keep me up at night.

Sometimes I don't know exactly where my fingers are placed *on* an object—maybe due to poor localization, wonky proprioception, or both; it's impossible to say. Once, eyes on my Kindle, I attempted a lusty bite from the sandwich I was holding in my right hand and got a mouthful of my own digits instead. I hadn't known my fingers were so close to the mouth-edge of my sandwich, or that implicitly knowing where your fingers are on a sandwich is key to safe mouth placement. Damn, human incisors are good! Though overkill on an egg-mayo sarnie. Now, I always look before I bite.

In addition to making me more vulnerable to physical injury, these sensory eccentricities render me somewhere between hapless and hopeless at tasks requiring fine dexterity—tying shoelaces, screwing jar lids on, opening crisp packets, finding correct change in my pocket, and the like. Fumbling at sex like a novice made me realize just how much fine dexterity it involves. But it's not really the sort of thing you bring up when your hand therapist says, "What else do you need to be able to do?"

At the root of all these issues lies a seriously weakened

central/peripheral nervous system feedback loop. With my median nerve delivering poor information about the location, nature, and intensity of stimuli in my environment, the central nervous system struggles to craft appropriate motor responses for my hand. "Garbage in, garbage out," as a former boss used to say, explaining how poor briefing led to poor work product. Why is this the case? I'm going to call it Murphy's Law of Peripheral Axon Regeneration: Everything that could have gone wrong—and, remember, the list of possibilities is very long—probably did, to some degree.

If true, then my median nerve now transmits *less* environmental data, because some axons haven't regenerated, and those that did regenerate transmit data more slowly, because they are less well-insulated than a pristine axon. The median nerve also transmits a distorted mix of environmental data, because axons transmitting about different types of stimuli (thermal, mechanical, chemical, etc.) did not regenerate with similar success. And then, the transmissions themselves have changed in format, and the central nervous system must learn how to interpret them. This requires the remodeling of trillions of connections between neurons, as well as between peripheral axons and their target cells; for reasons neuroscientists still don't understand, this doesn't happen fully or well.

But I've truly buried the lede here, which is that one way or another, I can do everything I need to. Sometimes a task just takes modifying to perform effectively. For example, I can manipulate writing and eating utensils perfectly well if I hold them between the middle and ring fingers of my right hand, instead of my index and middle fingers the way I used to. That works because I have a bit of light-touch sensation in my ring finger, whereas my middle finger is completely numb.

I now lock and unlock my front door with my left hand because I can't feel the give and take of the lock mechanism through the key when I'm holding it in my right hand (yeah, there's a special sensory receptor for that) and couldn't find a way to overcome that deficit. But because my left hand hasn't had the benefit of a lifetime of motor babbling with a key ring, it's not great at the job, either. So I get a little lesson in patience, coming and going from home every day.

When modification doesn't work, I allow more time to struggle through a task (please don't hold my coat for me; it takes me ages to feel my way into the right sleeve if I'm not holding it myself). Or I delegate it to other people. A big shout-out to all the women colleagues who have lent their sensory receptors when I needed necklaces, left-cuff buttons, and dress zippers fastened.

Even when my right hand can do a mechanical job, I'll use my left if texture is the point, like when I want to appreciate the rough bark of some ancient tree my mates and I pass on a country run, or the soft, nubby yarn my mother chose for the cowl she knit me last winter. Caressing and hair tousling are left-handed tasks, too; they're meant to bond, and their power seems diluted if they only generate pleasing outbound sensations.

Alas, led by my left hand, such tactile experiences still don't feel as rich as I remember them being when led by my right. And as I recall, my right hand was always better than my left at this kind of fine-texture discrimination. I suppose a dearth of motor babbling is implicated here, too. Do I miss having a fully receptive dominant hand? Do I miss the pleasure flood of perceiving the richest, most lovely tactile sensations in stereo? I didn't, until I started exploring the matter for this chapter. Ah well, I'll get over it.

While I'd once feared discovering some meaningful activity that my impaired hand prevented me from doing, deep into one of England's severe COVID-19 lockdowns, I found instead that I could do more with it than I'd ever hoped.

Worn down by isolation, and throbbing with anger and grief about the pandemic, and about corrupt politics and deadly racial injustice roiling in America, I was working hard to maintain emotional equilibrium. Running, meditating, and video chatting with loved ones offered some relief, but not enough. Then, during one of those "I have no right to complain, but . . ." conversations so frequent at the time, my friend Gadi suggested some self-care I hadn't considered.

"What are you doing for fun?" he asked. It felt slightly indecent to consider fun while the world was on fire. But not being Jesus, I'm well aware that my suffering doesn't reduce anyone else's, and by golly I wanted to reduce mine. I mentally sifted through a heap of recent time, tossing aside all the ugly bits to find moments of communion, kindness, and pleasure. The thought of them briefly warmed me, but nothing I unearthed even approached the lighthearted, rejuvenating experience of fun. Aside from writing this book—which, given the subject matter, was also often emotionally taxing—everything I was doing counted as coping.

"Nothing," I replied. "There is absolutely no fun in my life."

"That's a big problem, Becca. What are you going to do about it?"

A few weeks later, I took my first online Scottish fiddle lesson. Researching the genre on a whim, I'd discovered more than enough reasons to give it a try. A lot of Scottish fiddle music is written to mimic bagpipes, whose whining, melancholic drone I've always loved. It also benefited, by association, from my fondness for other Scottish products, including a good friend who helped make London home for me, the Edinburgh Festival Fringe, the campy *Highlander* movies, and die-hard Scotland football fans who wear kilts to matches. The matter-of-factness of the tune names, like "Mrs. MacLeod of Raasay" and "Jenny Dang the Weaver," really crack me up for some reason. And most important, as a folk-playing rookie, I wouldn't mind sucking at it.

My classical violin technique was surprisingly easy to coax out of retirement, and has proved useful in learning fiddle, as both types of music are played on the same instrument. Also, I needn't have worried about my right-hand impairments. The alternative bow grip Connie suggested initially felt awkward, but it feels so natural now that my hand automatically assumes the shape of it when I reach for my bow—and my wobbly pinky doesn't set me back as much as I thought it would. Many expert fiddlers don't even touch their little fingers to the bow. I still drop it sometimes, and so far, I can't help making a slight crunch sound when changing bow direction on the lower strings. But my teacher says the sound is a sought-after characteristic of "dirty" Cape Breton fiddling, and I choose to believe her.

Fiddle music is rhythmically and melodically distinct from anything I've ever played—pulsing, hiccupping, noodling, and swooping in ways that continually defy my expectations; riddled with tricky syncopation; and embellished with finger-snapping "cuts," bow-shivering "birls," and other funky ornaments that have no classical equivalents. So I've got my motor babbling cut out for me.

An even bigger challenge is learning what's not on the page—the spirit of the music that makes it folk, and Scottish, which someone growing up in Glasgow or Skye would have absorbed from the language, culture, and landscape in which they're immersed. When I've got bow well in hand, I instinctively play with a Western classical music sensibility, which is characteristically smooth and precise—not at all what the gritty, foot-stomping jigs, reels, and strathspeys that I'm learning want. Imagine an opera singer belting out Beyoncé's "Single Ladies (Put a Ring on It)" and you get the picture. But I'm starting to catch the Scottish groove, and learning the music is a delight. In applying myself to it, I've also pleased Connie and Dr. Vargas, both instrumental in enabling my new passion in their very different ways.

I live in a modest, outer-London borough, in what might best be described as a mews, except that the small Victorian row houses are arranged on either side of an overgrown common garden instead of pavement. I practice fiddle standing in front of my bedroom window, which overlooks my postage-stamp garden, the common garden, and my neighbors' houses opposite me, mirror images of my own.

There's always something to watch while I practice. An amazing array of birds flock to our trees and feeders throughout the day—including, depending on the season, city pigeons, wood pigeons, magpies, crows, robins, jays, starlings, sparrows, tits, blackbirds, parakeets, and goldfinches—while gulls, swallows, and the occasional peregrine falcon shriek above. My neighbors walk by with workbags, baby strollers, and grocery sacks; their small children chase each other up and down the walk; and their well-fed cats dot the gardens, mostly preferring napping to bird hunting. When the humans disappear, bats swoop in, and urban foxes trot around looking for carelessly bagged rubbish to raid and scatter about.

I practice with the windows open when it's warm, and the resident seven-year-old is my biggest (perhaps only) fan. She'll wave up to me, rope her friends into a little dance-off if I'm playing something jaunty, and occasionally make requests.

"We have to bury a snail. Can you play something sad?" she asked recently. I complied with "They Stole My Wife from Me Last Night," an eighteenth-century tune that is sad indeed, if the referenced event really happened.

For my own pleasure, I keep coming back to "A Happy Day in June," a lilting contemporary tune by Lauren MacColl that rocks gently back and forth across the strings, asking mostly for sweetness but also for a satisfying bit of digging in the lower registers. It accompanies my bedroom view like a good movie soundtrack, drawing attention to what matches its tone, brightening even a bleak-weather day. My fingers know the music now, so that when I play it, I mostly forget myself. When intermittently aware, I feel whole, and a part of everything.

ACKNOWLEDGMENTS

This book, like my replant surgery, was an aligning of stars, and I'd like to express my deepest gratitude to the many people who shifted them on my behalf, including:

Felicity Rubenstein, my agent, for betting on and advocating for me from start to finish. Caroline Sutton and Laura Barber, my editors at Avery (US) and Granta (UK), respectively, for embracing my vision and, with keen insight and sensitivity, helping me deliver on it. Kim Witherspoon at InkWell Management for opening the door to North American readers.

The extended teams at Avery and Granta for easy collaboration and beautiful results in producing and launching the book, and Julie Unruh for *Becca's Next Life Begins Now*—the breathtaking painting reproduced opposite the title page.

All those who so generously and enthusiastically shared their expertise, via interviews, draft reviews, and more: Charles L. Bardes, professor of clinical medicine, Weill Cornell Medicine; Alycia Bartley-Heinsen, clinical instructor of psychiatry and behavioral sciences, George Washington University School of Medicine; George A. Bonanno, professor of clinical psychology, Teachers College, Columbia University; Dario Farina, professor and chair in neurorehabilitation engineering, Imperial College London; Roberto L. Flores, Joseph G. McCarthy associate professor of reconstructive plastic surgery,

NYU Grossman School of Medicine; Andrew D. Gaudet, assistant professor of psychology and neurology, University of Texas at Austin; Guy Glover, consultant in critical care and anesthesia, Guy's and St. Thomas' NHS Foundation Trust; Johannes Gräff, associate professor of neuroscience at École Polytechnique Fédérale de Lausanne; Gareth Grier, consultant in emergency medicine and pre-hospital care, Barts Health NHS Trust and London's Air Ambulance; Martin P. Griffiths, CBE, DL, consultant vascular and trauma surgeon, Barts Health NHS Trust; Angela E. Kedgley, reader in orthopedic biomechanics, Imperial College London; Joseph E. LeDoux, professor of neural science and psychology, New York University; Steve K. Lee, chief of hand and upper extremity surgery service, Hospital for Special Surgery; David J. Linden, professor of neuroscience, Johns Hopkins University School of Medicine; Emily Mayhew, military medical historian in residence, Imperial College London; Vivek Muthurangu, professor of cardiac imaging and physics, University College London; Lt. Col. Claire Park, MBE, Royal Army Medical Corps, consultant in anesthesia, critical care, and pre-hospital care, King's College Hospital and London's Air Ambulance; Elizabeth Payumo, occupational therapist, certified hand therapist; David C. Rubin, professor of psychology and neuroscience, Duke University; Parviz L. Sadigh, consultant plastic surgeon, Barts Health NHS Trust; Daniela Schiller, professor of psychiatry and neuroscience, Icahn School of Medicine at Mount Sinai; Hunter Schone, PhD candidate in neuroscience, University College

London and National Institutes of Mental Health; Steven Southwick, professor emeritus of psychiatry, Yale School of Medicine; Agnes Sturma, associate researcher in bioengineering at Imperial College London; Julian Thompson, consultant in intensive care and anesthesia at North Bristol NHS Trust; Paolo Valenti, MD; Marc E. Walker, assistant professor of plastic surgery and orthopedic Surgery, University of Mississippi Medical Center; Carol Ward, professor of pathology and anatomical sciences, University of Missouri School of Medicine; Mark H. Wilson, consultant neurosurgeon at Imperial College Healthcare NHS Trust; Michelle Winslow, oral historian and qualitative researcher in supportive and palliative care, University of Sheffield; Clifford Woolf, professor of neurology, Harvard Medical School; and Adam Zeman, professor of cognitive and behavioral neurology, University of Exeter. Any errors in these pages related to their specialties are entirely mine.

Jennifer Brown, Lara Constable, and Julia Fuller-Nakayama for thought-provoking and meaningful comments on my first complete draft. The Royal Society of Literature for recognizing my work-in-progress with a 2019 Giles St. Aubyn Award—Judges' Special Commendation. The staff and communities of the London Library, the British Library, Bibliothèque Mazarine, Bibliothèque Sainte-Geneviève, Wellcome Collection, London Writers' Salon, Caveday.com, and Blue Belle Café for glorious and supportive spaces in which to work.

Michael Bond, Adrienne Brodeur, Victoria Hislop, and Emily Mayhew for above-and-beyond mentoring and advocacy in the process and business of writing and—along with Ron Balzan, Victoria Preston, Victor Sebestyen, Diana Souhami, and Kassia St. Clair—creative inspiration and fellowship. The late Clayton Christensen for early opportunities to hone my craft, and Karen Dillon, Hayden Hill, and Tina Ross for helping me do so.

Finally, to my extended Bellevue care team, especially "Dr. Vargas" and "Beth," as well as Janet Baird, MD, for great skill and compassion in treating my wounds; and to all my dear ones—many of whom appear above and throughout these pages, and others who I hope recognize themselves as such—for their love, acceptance, care, and encouragement, particularly during my recovery and the writing of this book. You are the beauty in trauma, and in joy.

BIBLIOGRAPHY

While many sources informed my writing throughout the book, I have cited each in the chapter most closely aligned with its topic. Please see the acknowledgments for a list of the experts I interviewed.

2. FIGHT OR FLIGHT? OUR BUILT-IN THREAT-DEFENSE PROGRAM

Berntsen, Dorthe, and Annette Bohn. "Remembering and Forecasting: The Relation Between Autobiographical Memory and Episodic Future Thinking." *Memory & Cognition* 38, no. 3 (April 1, 2010): 265–78.

Cancio, Colleen. "How Tankless Toilets Work." HowStuffWorks, April 16, 2021. Web.

Eagleman, David. *The Brain: The Story of You.* Edinburgh: Canongate, 2015.

Exley, Christine L., and Judd B. Kessler. "The Gender Gap in Self-Promotion." Working Paper. National Bureau of Economic Research, October 2019.

Fernyhough, Charles. *Pieces of Light: The New Science of Memory.* London: Profile, 2012.

Harvard Extension School. "Action Potential in the Neuron." 2018. YouTube video, 13:12.

Hasudungan, Armando. "Neurology - Neuron." Armando Hasudungan Biology and Medicine Videos, 2013. YouTube video, 11:21.

LeDoux, Joseph E. *Anxious: Using the Brain to Understand and Treat Fear and Anxiety.* New York: Penguin, 2016.

LeDoux, Joseph E. *The Deep History of Ourselves: The Four-Billion-Year Story of How We Got Conscious Brains.* New York: Viking, 2019.

LeDoux, Joseph E. *The Emotional Brain: The Mysterious Underpinnings of Emotional Life.* London: Phoenix, 2003.

LeDoux, Joseph E. "'Run, Hide, Fight' Is Not How Our Brains Work." *New York Times,* December 18, 2015, sec. Opinion.

LeDoux, Joseph E. "Semantics, Surplus Meaning, and the Science of Fear." *Trends in Cognitive Sciences* 21, no. 5 (May 2017): 303–6.

LeDoux, Joseph E., and Daniel S. Pine. "Using Neuroscience to Help Understand Fear and Anxiety: A Two-System Framework." *American Journal of Psychiatry* 173, no. 11 (November 1, 2016): 1083–93.

LeDoux, Joseph E., and Nathaniel D. Daw. "Surviving Threats: Neural Circuit and Computational Implications of a New Taxonomy of Defensive Behaviour." *Nature Reviews Neuroscience* 19, no. 5 (May 2018): 269–82.

LeDoux, Joseph E., and Richard Brown. "A Higher-Order Theory of Emotional Consciousness." *Proceedings of the National Academy of Sciences* 114, no. 10 (March 7, 2017): E2016–25.

LeDoux, Joseph E., Matthias Michel, and Hakwan Lau. "A Little History Goes a Long Way Toward Understanding Why We Study Consciousness the Way We Do Today." *Proceedings of the National Academy of Sciences* 117, no. 13 (March 31, 2020): 6976–84.

LeDoux, Joseph, Richard Brown, Daniel Pine, and Stefan Hofmann. "Know Thyself: Well-Being and Subjective Experience." *Cerebrum: The Dana Forum on Brain Science* 2018 (February 2018): cer-01-18.

Machalinski, Anne. "Hypovolemic Shock." WebMD, April 30, 2020.

Mayo Clinic. "Shock: First Aid." April 29, 2021. Web.

Moss-Racusin, Corinne, and Laurie Rudman. "Disruptions in Women's Self-Promotion: The Backlash Avoidance Model." *Psychology of Women Quarterly* 34, no. 2 (May 6, 2010): 186–202.

Oosterwijk, Suzanne, Kristen A. Lindquist, Eric Anderson, Rebecca Dautoff, Yoshiya Moriguchi, and Lisa Feldman Barrett. "States of Mind: Emotions, Body Feelings, and Thoughts Share Distributed Neural Networks." *NeuroImage* 62, no. 3 (September 2012): 2110–28.

Pettus, Ashley. "What Makes the Human Mind?" *Harvard Magazine*, November 1, 2008.

Rubin, David C. "Placing Autobiographical Memory in a General Memory Organization." In John H. Mace, ed., *The Organization and Structure of Autobiographical Memory*. Oxford: Oxford University Press, 2019.

Schacter, Daniel L. *Searching for Memory: The Brain, the Mind, and the Past*. New York: Basic Books, 1996.

Sharma, Ragav, and Sandeep Sharma. "Physiology, Blood Volume." In *StatPearls [Internet]*. Treasure Island, FL: StatPearls, 2022.

Watson, Stephanie. "Blood Glucose (Blood Sugar): How It's Made, How It's Used, Healthy Levels." WebMD, June 13, 2020.

Zeman, Adam. *Consciousness: A User's Guide*. New Haven, CT: Yale University Press, 2004.

Zeman, Adam. "What Do We Mean by 'Conscious' and 'Aware'?" *Neuropsychological Rehabilitation* 16, no. 4 (August 1, 2006): 356–76.

Zeman, Adam. "What in the World Is Consciousness?" In *The Boundaries of Consciousness: Neurobiology and Neuropathology*, edited by Steven Laureys, 1–10. Vol. 150 of *Progress in Brain Research*. Elsevier, 2005.

Zeman, Adam, Matthew MacKisack, and John Onians. "The Eye's Mind - Visual Imagination, Neuroscience and the Humanities." *Cortex* 105 (August 2018): 1–3.

4. INSTRUMENT OF INSTRUMENTS: ANATOMY OF THE HAND

Angier, Natalie. "Each Flick of a Digit Is a Job for All 5." *New York Times*, February 27, 2012, sec. Science.

Bibliography

Bartleby.com: Great Books Online. "Gray, Henry. 1918. Anatomy of the Human Body." 2000.

Brock, Oliver, and Francisco Valero-Cuevas. "Transferring Synergies from Neuroscience to Robotics: Comment on 'Hand Synergies.'" *Physics of Life Reviews* 17 (July 2016): 27–32.

Carmel, David, and Daniela Schiller. "How Free Is Your Will?" *Scientific American*, March 22, 2011.

Corballis, Michael C. *The Recursive Mind: The Origins of Human Language, Thought, and Civilization*. Princeton, NJ: Princeton University Press, 2011.

Costandi, Mo. "Brainy Processing at Your Fingertips." *The Guardian*, September 8, 2014, sec. Science.

Eagleman, David. *Incognito: The Secret Lives of the Brain*. New York: Pantheon Books, 2011.

Farina, Dario. "The Bionic Man: Interfacing the Human Nervous System with Robotic Limbs." Presented at Imperial College London, December 7, 2016. YouTube video, 46:37.

Farina, Dario, Francesco Negro, Silvia Muceli, and Roger M. Enoka. "Principles of Motor Unit Physiology Evolve with Advances in Technology." *Physiology* 31, no. 2 (March 2016): 83–94.

Flinn, Mark V., David C. Geary, and Carol V. Ward. "Ecological Dominance, Social Competition, and Coalitionary Arms Races: Why Humans Evolved Extraordinary Intelligence." *Evolution and Human Behavior* 26, no. 1 (January 1, 2005): 10–46.

Francis, Gavin. *Adventures in Human Being*. London: Wellcome Collection, 2016.

Gesslbauer, Bernhard, Laura Hruby, Aidan Roche, Dario Farina, Roland Blumer, and Oskar Aszmann. "Axonal Components of Nerves Innervating the Human Arm." *Annals of Neurology* 82, no. 3 (August 18, 2017): 396–408.

Hahne, Janne, Meike Wilke, Mario Koppe, and Dario Farina. "Simultaneous Control of Multiple Functions of Bionic Hand Prostheses." *Science Robotics* 3, no. 19 (June 20, 2018): eaat3630.

Hasudungan, Armando. "Introduction to How Reflexes Work." Armando Hasudungan Biology and Medicine Videos, 2019. YouTube video, 14:24.

Hasudungan, Armando. "Neurology - Motor Pathways." Armando Hasudungan Biology and Medicine Videos, 2015. YouTube video, 12:31.

Hasudungan, Armando. "Sensory Tracts." Armando Hasudungan Biology and Medicine Videos, 2018. YouTube video, 8:50.

Hasudungan, Armando. "Spinal Cord - Clinical Anatomy and Physiology." Armando Hasudungan Biology and Medicine Videos, 2019. YouTube video, 22:18.

Institute for Quality and Efficiency in Health Care. "How Do Hands Work?" InformedHealth.org. Cologne, Germany: Institute for Quality and Efficiency in Health Care (IQWiG), 2018.

Jones, Edward G. "The Sensory Hand." *Brain* 129, no. 12 (December 1, 2006): 3413–20.

Latash, Mark, John Scholz, and Gregor Schöner. "Toward a New Theory of Motor Synergies." *Motor Control* 11, no. 3 (August 1, 2007): 276–308.

Leo, Andrea, Giacomo Handjaras, Matteo Bianchi, Hamal Marino, Marco Gabiccini, Andrea Guidi, Enzo Pasquale Scilingo, et al. "A Synergy-Based Hand Control Is Encoded in Human Motor Cortical Areas." *ELife* 5 (n.d.): e13420.

Linden, David J. *Touch: The Science of Hand, Heart and Mind.* New York: Viking, 2015.

Maurette, Pablo. "The Children of Anaxagoras." *Lapham's Quarterly*, July 9, 2018.

Napier, John Russell, and Russell H. Tuttle. *Hands*, rev. ed. Princeton Science Library. Princeton, NJ: Princeton University Press, 1993.

Roberts, Michelle. "Ancient Hand Bone Dates Origins of Human Dexterity." BBC News, December 17, 2013. Web.

Santello, Marco, Matteo Bianchi, Marco Gabiccini, Emiliano Ricciardi, Gionata Salvietti, Domenico Prattichizzo, Marc Ernst, et al. "Hand Synergies: Integration of Robotics and Neuroscience for Understanding the Control of Biological and Artificial Hands." *Physics of Life Reviews* 17, no. 17 (July 2016): 1–23.

Solly, Meilan. "Did the Human Hand Evolve as a Lean Mean Bone-Smashing Machine?" *Smithsonian*, July 13, 2018.

Ward, Carol V., Matthew W. Tocheri, J. Michael Plavcan, Francis H. Brown, and Fredrick Kyalo Manthi. "Early Pleistocene Third Metacarpal from Kenya and the Evolution of Modern Human-like Hand Morphology." *Proceedings of the National Academy of Sciences* 111, no. 1 (January 7, 2014): 121–24.

Wilson, Frank R. *The Hand.* New York: Random House International; London: Hi Marketing, 2000.

6. BIG-WAVE SURFING: REPLANTING A PARTIALLY AMPUTATED HAND

American Board of Surgery. "Specialty of Hand Surgery Defined." n.d. Web.

American Trauma Society. "Trauma Center Levels Explained." n.d. Web.

Battiston, Bruno, Igor Papalia, Pierluigi Tos, and Stefano Geuna. "Chapter 1: Peripheral Nerve Repair and Regeneration Research: A Historical Note." *International Review of Neurobiology* 87 (February 2009): 1–7.

Beasley, Robert W. *Beasley's Surgery of the Hand.* New York: Thieme, 2003.

Boyes, Joseph H. *On the Shoulders of Giants: Notable Names in Hand Surgery.* Philadelphia: Lippincott, 1976.

British Library. "Letter from Frances Burney to Her Sister Esther About Her Mastectomy Without Anaesthetic, 1812." n.d. Web.

British Society for Surgery of the Hand. "Our History." n.d. Web.

Bunnell, Sterling. *Bunnell's Surgery of the Hand*, 3rd ed. Philadelphia: Lippincott, 1964.

Bunnell, Sterling, ed. *Hand Surgery in World War II.* Washington, DC: Office of the Surgeon General, Department of the Army, 1955.

Carter, Peter R. "The Embryogenesis of the Specialty of Hand Surgery: A Story of Three Great Americans—a Politician, a General, and a Duck Hunter: The 2002

Richard J. Smith Memorial Lecture." *Journal of Hand Surgery* 28, no. 2 (March 1, 2003): 185–98.

Cleveland, Mathur, ed. *Orthopedic Surgery in the European Theater of Operations.* Washington, DC: Office of the Surgeon General, Department of the Army, 1956.

Elizondo-Omaña, Rodrigo E., Santos Guzmán-López, and María De Los Angeles García-Rodríguez. "Dissection as a Teaching Tool: Past, Present, and Future." *The Anatomical Record Part B: The New Anatomist* 285B, no. 1 (2005): 11–15.

Feliciano, David V., Kenneth L. Mattox, and Ernest Eugene Moore, eds. *Trauma*, 6th ed. New York: McGraw-Hill Medical, 2008.

Freiberg, Jeffrey A. "The Mythos of Laudable Pus Along with an Explanation for Its Origin." *Journal of Community Hospital Internal Medicine Perspectives* 7, no. 3 (July 13, 2017): 196–98.

Gaynes, Robert. "The Discovery of Penicillin—New Insights After More Than 75 Years of Clinical Use." *Emerging Infectious Diseases* 23, no. 5 (May 2017): 849–53.

Ghosh, Sanjib Kumar. "Human Cadaveric Dissection: A Historical Account from Ancient Greece to the Modern Era." *Anatomy & Cell Biology* 48, no. 3 (September 2015): 153–69.

Giannou, Christos, and Marco Baldan. *War Surgery: Working with Limited Resources in Armed Conflict and Other Situations of Violence*, vol. 1. Geneva: International Committee of the Red Cross, 2009.

Green, Stuart A. "Giants in Orthopaedic Surgery: Sterling Bunnell MD." *Clinical Orthopaedics and Related Research* 471, no. 12 (December 2013): 3750–54.

Griffin, M., S. Hindocha, D. Jordan, M. Saleh, and W. Khan. "An Overview of the Management of Flexor Tendon Injuries." *Open Orthopaedics Journal* 6 (February 23, 2012): 28–35.

Grinsell, D., and C. P. Keating. "Peripheral Nerve Reconstruction After Injury: A Review of Clinical and Experimental Therapies." *BioMed Research International* 2014, no. 4 (September 2014): 698256.

Hanigan, William. "The Development of Military Medical Care for Peripheral Nerve Injuries During World War I." *Neurosurgical Focus* 28, no. 5 (May 2010): E24.

Hawk, Alan James. "How Hemorrhage Control Became Common Sense." *Journal of Trauma and Acute Care Surgery* 85, no. 1S, suppl. 2 (July 2018): S13–17.

Hepburn, Brian, and Hanne Andersen. "Scientific Method." In *The Stanford Encyclopedia of Philosophy*, edited by Edward N. Zalta, summer 2021. Metaphysics Research Lab, Stanford University, 2021.

Hodgetts, Tim, and Lee Turner. *Trauma Rules 2: Incorporating Military Trauma Rules*, 2nd ed. Malden, MA: Blackwell, 2006.

Hollingham, Richard. *Blood and Guts: A History of Surgery*. London: BBC Books, 2008.

Hovius, Steven, and Ton Schreuders. "Spaghetti Wrist Trauma: Functional Recovery, Return to Work, and Psychological Effects." *Plastic and Reconstructive Surgery*, January 1, 2005.

Johns Hopkins Medicine. "Surgical Site Infections." n.d. Web.

Kleinert Kutz Hand Care Center. "Our History." n.d. Web.

Bibliography

Kneebone, Roger. "The Art of War." *The Lancet* 384, no. 9955 (November 8, 2014): 1662–63.

Levinthal, R., W. J. Brown, and R. W. Rand. "Comparison of Fascicular, Interfascicular and Epineural Suture Techniques in the Repair of Simple Nerve Lacerations." *Journal of Neurosurgery* 47, no. 5 (November 1977): 744–50.

MacKinnon, Susan E. "Strategies of Peripheral Nerve Surgery." WUSTL Learn Surgery, October 2, 2018. YouTube video, 53:00.

Majno, Guido, MD. *The Healing Hand: Man and Wound in the Ancient World.* Cambridge, MA: Harvard University Press, 1975.

Manring, M. M., Alan Hawk, Jason H. Calhoun, and Romney C. Andersen. "Treatment of War Wounds: A Historical Review." *Clinical Orthopaedics and Related Research* 467, no. 8 (August 2009): 2168–91.

Manske, Paul R. "History of Flexor Tendon Repair." *Hand Clinics* 21, no. 2 (May 2005): 123–27.

Mavrogenis, Andreas F., Konstantinos Markatos, Theodosis Saranteas, Ioannis Ignatiadis, Sarantis Spyridonos, Marko Bumbasirevic, Alexandru Valentin Georgescu, Alexandros Beris, and Panayotis N. Soucacos. "The History of Microsurgery." *European Journal of Orthopaedic Surgery & Traumatology* 29, no. 2 (February 1, 2019): 247–54.

Mayhew, Emily. *A Heavy Reckoning: War, Medicine and Survival in Afghanistan and Beyond.* London: Profile Books Wellcome Collection, 2018.

Mayo Clinic. "Gangrene - Symptoms and Causes." n.d. Web.

McClellan, Thomas, MD. "Flexor Tendon Exploration and Repair Palm." McClellan Plastic Surgery, 2018. YouTube video, 8:12.

McClellan, Thomas, MD. "Live Surgery: Tendon Repair Hand/Finger Kessler Technique." McClellan Plastic Surgery, 2015. YouTube video, 3:15.

Meals, Clifton G., and James Chang. "Ten Tips to Simplify the Spaghetti Wrist." *Plastic and Reconstructive Surgery Global Open* 6, no. 12 (December 12, 2018): e1971.

Newmeyer, William L. "Sterling Bunnell, MD: The Founding Father." *Journal of Hand Surgery* 28, no. 1 (January 2003): 161–64.

NYC Health+Hospitals. "About Bellevue." n.d. Web.

Oshinsky, David M. *Bellevue: Three Centuries of Medicine and Mayhem at America's Most Storied Hospital.* New York: Doubleday, 2016.

Phillips, James, ed. *Trauma, Repair, and Recovery.* Introducing Health Sciences. Oxford: Oxford University Press; Milton Keynes, UK: Open University, 2008.

Porter, Roy. *Blood and Guts: A Short History of Medicine.* London: Allen Lane, 2002.

Science Museum. "Hospital Infection." n.d. Web.

Science Museum. "The Art of Anaesthesia." October 26, 2018. Web.

Science Museum. "War and Medicine." n.d. Web.

Sebastin, Sandeep J., Allison Ho, Teemu Karjalainen, and Kevin C. Chung. "History and Evolution of the Kessler Repair." *Journal of Hand Surgery* 38, no. 3 (March 2013): 552–61.

Siemionow, Maria, and Grzegorz Brzezicki. "Chapter 8: Current Techniques and Concepts in Peripheral Nerve Repair." *International Review of Neurobiology* 87 (February 2009): 141–72.

Urbaniak, James R., ed. *Hand Surgery Worldwide: International Reconstruction of a "Beautiful and Ready Instrument of the Mind."* Athens, Greece: Konstantaras Medical Publications, 2011.

van de Laar, Arnold. *Under the Knife: A History of Surgery in 28 Remarkable Operations.* London: John Murray, 2018.

Verano, John W., and Stanley Finger. "Ancient Trepanation." In *History of Neurology*, edited by Michael J. Aminoff, François Boller, and Dick F. Swaab, 3–14. Vol. 95 of *Handbook of Clinical Neurology*. Elsevier, 2009.

Verdan, C. "The History of Hand Surgery in Europe." *Journal of Hand Surgery: British & European Volume* 25, no. 3 (June 2000): 238–41.

Welling, David R., Patricia L. McKay, Todd E. Rasmussen, and Norman M. Rich. "A Brief History of the Tourniquet." *Journal of Vascular Surgery* 55, no. 1 (January 1, 2012): 286–90.

Whelan, Lynsay R., and Jeremy Farley. "Functional Outcomes with Externally Powered Partial Hand Prostheses." *JPO: Journal of Prosthetics and Orthotics* 30, no. 2 (April 2018): 69–73.

Wilson, William C., Christopher M. Grande, and David B. Hoyt. *Trauma: Emergency Resuscitation, Perioperative Anesthesia, Surgical Management*, vol. 1. New York: Informa Healthcare, 2007.

Wood Library-Museum of Anesthesiology. "History of Anesthesia." n.d. Web.

Wright, John. *A History of War Surgery.* Stroud, UK: Amberley, 2011.

8. WITH RESPECT TO PAIN: HOW IT HELPS AND WORKS

Brooks, Jonathan, and Irene Tracey. "From Nociception to Pain Perception: Imaging the Spinal and Supraspinal Pathways." *Journal of Anatomy* 207, no. 1 (July 2005): 19–33.

Brown, Emery, Ralph Lydic, and Nicholas Schiff. "General Anesthesia, Sleep, and Coma." *New England Journal of Medicine* 363, no. 27 (December 1, 2010): 2638–50.

Cole-Adams, Kate. *Anesthesia: The Gift of Oblivion and the Mystery of Consciousness.* Berkeley: Counterpoint Press, 2017.

Dafny, Nachum, PhD. "Pain Principles (Section 2, Chapter 6)." In *Neuroscience Online: An Electronic Textbook for the Neurosciences.* University of Texas Medical School at Houston, October 7, 2020.

Davidhizar, R., and J. N. Giger. "A Review of the Literature on Care of Clients in Pain Who Are Culturally Diverse." *International Nursing Review* 51, no. 1 (March 2004): 47–55.

Dunbar, Robin, Kostas Kaskatis, Ian MacDonald, and Vincent Barra. "Performance of Music Elevates Pain Threshold and Positive Affect." *Evolutionary Psychology* 10, no. 4 (October 1, 2012): 688–702.

Ferdousi, Mehnaz, and David Finn. "Stress-Induced Modulation of Pain: Role of the Endogenous Opioid System." In *The Opioid System as the Interface Between the Brain's Cognitive and Motivational Systems*, edited by Shane O'Mara, 121–77. Vol. 239 of *Progress in Brain Research*. Elsevier, 2018.

Bibliography

Geddes, Linda. "Banishing Consciousness: The Mystery of Anaesthesia." *New Scientist*, November 23, 2011.

Glovin, Bill. "Finding the Hurt in Pain - With Irene Tracey, PhD." *Cerebrum*, February 13, 2017. Podcast, 41:00.

Hasudungan, Armando. "Nociceptors - An Introduction to Pain." Armando Hasudungan Biology and Medicine Videos, 2013. YouTube video, 12:17.

Hasudungan, Armando. "PAIN! Physiology - The Ascending Pathway." Armando Hasudungan Biology and Medicine Videos, 2018. YouTube video, 8:14.

Hasudungan, Armando. "Part I - Inflammation." Armando Hasudungan Biology and Medicine Videos, 2013. YouTube video, 8:27.

Hasudungan, Armando. "Part II - Inflammation." Armando Hasudungan Biology and Medicine Videos, 2013. YouTube video, 7:54.

Institute of Medicine (US) Committee on Advancing Pain Research, Care, and Education. "Relieving Pain in America." Washington, DC: National Academies Press, 2011. Web.

"Is Pain an Emotion?" *BBC World Questions*, n.d. Radio broadcast, 49:45.

Jackson, Marni. *Pain: The Science and Culture of Why We Hurt*. London: Bloomsbury, 2003.

Kopp Lugli, Andrea, Charles Spencer Yost, and Christoph H. Kindler. "Anaesthetic Mechanisms: Update on the Challenge of Unravelling the Mystery of Anaesthesia." *European Journal of Anaesthesiology* 26, no. 10 (October 2009): 807–20.

Levitin, Daniel J. *This Is Your Brain on Music: The Science of a Human Obsession*. London: Plume Books, 2007.

Mayo Clinic. "How Opioid Addiction Occurs." n.d. Web.

Miller, Elaine T., and Dania M. Abu-Alhaija. "Cultural Influences on Pain Perception and Management." *Pain Management Nursing* 20, no. 3 (June 1, 2019): 183–84.

National Academies of Science, Engineering and Medicine. "IOM Report Calls for Cultural Transformation of Attitudes Toward Pain and Its Prevention and Management." June 29, 2011. Web.

NIH National Institute on Drug Abuse. "Drug Misuse and Addiction." July 13, 2020. Web.

NPR. "You Won't Feel a Thing: Your Brain on Anesthesia." April 25, 2011. Web.

Perkins, Bill. "How Does Anesthesia Work?" *Scientific American*, February 7, 2005.

Przybylo, Henry Jay. *Counting Backwards: A Doctor's Notes on Anesthesia*. New York: W. W. Norton, 2018.

Purves, Dale, George J. Augustine, David Fitzpatrick, Lawrence C. Katz, Anthony-Samuel LaMantia, James O. McNamara, and S. Mark Williams, eds. "Neuroscience." In *Nociceptors*, 2nd ed. Sunderland, MA: Sinauer Associates, 2001.

Thernstrom, Melanie. *The Pain Chronicles: Cures, Myths, Mysteries, Prayers, Diaries, Brain Scans, Healing, and the Science of Suffering*. New York: Picador, 2011.

Tracey, Irene. "Finding the Hurt in Pain." *Cerebrum: The Dana Forum on Brain Science* 2016 (December 1, 2016): cer-15-16.

Tracey, W. Daniel. "Nociception." *Current Biology* 27, no. 4 (February 20, 2017): R129–33.

Wiech, Katja, Markus Ploner, and Irene Tracey. "Neurocognitive Aspects of Pain Perception." *Trends in Cognitive Sciences* 12, no. 8 (August 2008): 306–13.

Woolf, Clifford J. "Dissecting out Mechanisms Responsible for Peripheral Neuropathic Pain." *Life Sciences* 74, no. 21 (April 9, 2004): 2605–10.

Woolf, Clifford J. *Neurobiology of Pain*. OPENPediatrics, 2016. YouTube video, 42:29.

Woolf, Clifford J. "What Is This Thing Called Pain?" *Journal of Clinical Investigation* 120, no. 11 (November 1, 2010): 3742–44.

Xu, Qinghao, and Tony L. Yaksh. "A Brief Comparison of the Pathophysiology of Inflammatory Versus Neuropathic Pain." *Current Opinion in Anaesthesiology* 24, no. 4 (August 2011): 400–407.

10. AFTER THE UNTHINKABLE: PSYCHOLOGICAL RECOVERY

American Psychiatric Association. "What Is PTSD?" n.d. Web.

Atwoli, Lukoye, Dan J. Stein, Karestan C. Koenen, and Katie A. McLaughlin. "Epidemiology of Posttraumatic Stress Disorder: Prevalence, Correlates and Consequences." *Current Opinion in Psychiatry* 28, no. 4 (July 2015): 307–11.

Benjet, C., E. Bromet, E. G. Karam, R. C. Kessler, K. A. McLaughlin, A. M. Ruscio, V. Shahly, et al. "The Epidemiology of Traumatic Event Exposure Worldwide: Results from the World Mental Health Survey Consortium." *Psychological Medicine* 46, no. 2 (January 2016): 327–43.

Berntsen, Dorthe, and David Rubin. "When a Trauma Becomes a Key to Identity: Enhanced Integration of Trauma Memories Predicts Posttraumatic Stress Disorder Symptoms." *Applied Cognitive Psychology* 21, no. 4 (May 1, 2007): 417–31.

Bonanno, George A. "Loss, Trauma, and Human Resilience: Have We Underestimated the Human Capacity to Thrive After Extremely Aversive Events?" *American Psychologist* 59, no. 1 (February 1, 2004): 20–28.

Bonanno, George A., and Anthony Mancini. "The Human Capacity to Thrive in the Face of Potential Trauma." *Pediatrics* 121, no. 2 (March 1, 2008): 369–75.

Bonanno, George A., Chris R. Brewin, Krzysztof Kaniasty, and Annette M. La Greca. "Weighing the Costs of Disaster: Consequences, Risks, and Resilience in Individuals, Families, and Communities." *Psychological Science in the Public Interest* 11, no. 1 (January 1, 2010): 1–49.

Bonanno, George A., Maren Westphal, and Anthony D. Mancini. "Resilience to Loss and Potential Trauma." *Annual Review of Clinical Psychology* 7, no. 1 (April 2010): 511–35.

Bond, Michael. "The Secrets of Extraordinary Survivors." BBC, August 14, 2015. Web.

Cave, Mark, and Stephen M. Sloan, eds. *Listening on the Edge: Oral History in the Aftermath of Crisis*. Oxford Oral History Series. New York: Oxford University Press, 2014.

Charon, Rita. "Narrative Reciprocity." *Hastings Center Report* 44, no. S1 (February 2014): S21–24.

Chen, Shuquan, and George Bonanno. "Psychological Adjustment During the Global Outbreak of COVID-19: A Resilience Perspective." *Psychological Trauma: Theory, Research, Practice, and Policy* 12 (June 15, 2020).

Clegg, Joshua W. "Teaching About Mental Health and Illness Through the History of the DSM." *History of Psychology* 15, no. 4 (November 2012): 364–70.

Collier, Lorna. "Growth After Trauma." American Psychological Society, November 2016. Web.

Collins, Francis S. *The Language of Life: DNA and the Revolution in Personalized Medicine*. New York: Harper, 2011.

Duane, Addison, Kimberly Stokes, Christina DeAngelis, and Erika Bocknek. "Collective Trauma and Community Support: Lessons from Detroit." *Psychological Trauma: Theory, Research, Practice, and Policy* 12, no. 5 (June 11, 2020): 452–54.

Field, Sean. "Beyond 'Healing': Trauma, Oral History and Regeneration." *Oral History* 34, no. 1 (2006): 31–42.

Frank, Arthur W. "The Standpoint of Storyteller." *Qualitative Health Research* 10, no. 3 (June 1, 2000): 354–65.

Frank, Arthur W. *The Wounded Storyteller: Body, Illness, and Ethics*. Chicago: University of Chicago Press, 1995.

Frank, Arthur W. "Why I Wrote . . . The Wounded Storyteller: A Recollection of Life and Ethics." *Clinical Ethics* 4, no. 2 (May 22, 2009): 106–8.

Friedman, Matthew J. "PTSD History and Overview." National Center for PTSD, US Department of Veterans Affairs, October 14, 2019. Web.

Galea, Sandro, David Vlahov, Heidi Resnick, Jennifer Ahern, Ezra Susser, Joel Gold, Michael Bucuvalas, and Dean Kilpatrick. "Trends of Probable Post-Traumatic Stress Disorder in New York City After the September 11 Terrorist Attacks." *American Journal of Epidemiology* 158, no. 6 (September 15, 2003): 514–24.

Gelernter, Joel. "The Epigenetics of Child Abuse." Yale School of Medicine, 2014. Web.

Gottschall, Jonathan. *The Storytelling Animal: How Stories Make Us Human*. Boston: Houghton Mifflin Harcourt, 2012.

Gottschall, Jonathan, and David Sloan Wilson, eds. *The Literary Animal: Evolution and the Nature of Narrative*. Evanston, IL: Northwestern University Press, 2005. BiblioVault.

Haslam, Sara. "Reading, Trauma and Literary Caregiving 1914–1918: Helen Mary Gaskell and the War Library." *Journal of Medical Humanities* 41, no. 3 (September 2020): 305–21.

Hathaway, Bill. "Brain Tissue Yields Clues to Causes of PTSD." YaleNews, December 21, 2020. Web.

Hathaway, Bill. "Nurture Trumps Nature in Determining Severity of PTSD Symptoms." YaleNews, October 1, 2020. Web.

Bibliography

Horn, Sarah R., and Adriana Feder. "Understanding Resilience and Preventing and Treating PTSD." *Harvard Review of Psychiatry* 26, no. 3 (June 2018): 158–74.

Hughes, Virginia. "Stress: The Roots of Resilience." *Nature* 490, no. 7419 (October 1, 2012): 165–67.

Hunt, Nigel, and Ian Robbins. "Telling Stories of the War: Ageing Veterans Coping with Their Memories Through Narrative." *Oral History* 26, no. 2 (1998): 57–64.

Kilpatrick, Dean G., Heidi S. Resnick, Melissa E. Milanak, Mark W. Miller, Katherine M. Keyes, and Matthew J. Friedman. "National Estimates of Exposure to Traumatic Events and PTSD Prevalence Using DSM-IV and DSM-5 Criteria." *Journal of Traumatic Stress* 26, no. 5 (October 2013): 537–47.

Klempner, Mark. "Navigating Life Review Interviews with Survivors of Trauma." *Oral History Review* 27, no. 2 (June 1, 2000): 67–83.

Mancini, Anthony. "Can Trauma Improve Our Psychological Health?" *Psychology Today*, July 16, 2016.

Mancini, Anthony. "The Trouble with Post-Traumatic Growth." *Psychology Today*, June 1, 2016.

Mancini, Anthony. "What Are the Psychological Harms of Disaster?" *Psychology Today*, October 24, 2017.

National Center for PTSD, US Department of Veterans Affairs. "How Common Is PTSD in Adults?" n.d. Web.

National Human Genome Research Institute. "Epigenetics." n.d. Web.

National Human Genome Research Institute. "Introduction to Genomics." n.d. Web.

New York University. "How Our Brains Remember 9/11. Elizabeth Phelps, Professor of Neuroscience." 2009. YouTube video, 6:22.

Normand, Lawrence. "Review of *Testimony: Crises of Witnessing in Literature, Psychoanalysis, and History*, by S. Felman and D. Laub." *Review of English Studies* 46, no. 181 (February 1995): 135–36.

Pai, Anushka, Alina M. Suris, and Carol S. North. "Posttraumatic Stress Disorder in the DSM-5: Controversy, Change, and Conceptual Considerations." *Behavioral Sciences* 7, no. 1 (February 13, 2017): 7.

Park, Crystal, Kristen Riley, and Leslie Snyder. "Meaning Making Coping, Making Sense, and Post-Traumatic Growth Following the 9/11 Terrorist Attacks." *Journal of Positive Psychology* 7, no. 3 (May 1, 2012): 1–10.

Parr, Alison. "Breaking the Silence: Traumatised War Veterans and Oral History." *Oral History* 35, no. 1 (Spring 2007): 61–70.

Reese, Elaine, Catherine Haden, Lynne Baker-Ward, Patricia Bauer, Robyn Fivush, and Peter Ornstein. "Coherence of Personal Narratives Across the Lifespan: A Multidimensional Model and Coding Method." *Journal of Cognition and Development: Official Journal of the Cognitive Development Society* 12, no. 4 (October 1, 2011): 424–62.

Rubin, David C. "A Basic Systems Account of Trauma Memories in PTSD: Is More Needed?" In *Clinical Perspectives on Autobiographical Memory*, edited by Dorthe Berntsen and Lynn A. Watson, 41–64. Cambridge: Cambridge University Press, 2015.

Bibliography

Rubin, David C. "Schema Driven Construction of Future Autobiographical Traumatic Events: The Future Is Much More Troubling Than the Past." *Journal of Experimental Psychology: General* 143, no. 2 (April 2014): 612–30.

Rubin, David C. "Self-Concept Focus: A Tendency to Perceive Autobiographical Events as Central to Identity." *Journal of Applied Research in Memory and Cognition* 9, no. 4 (December 2020): 576–86.

Sandberg, Sheryl, and Adam Grant. *Option B: Facing Adversity, Building Resilience and Finding Joy.* London: W. H. Allen, 2017.

Schiavone, Francesca, Paul Frewen, Margaret McKinnon, and Ruth A. Lanius. "The Dissociative Subtype of PTSD: An Update on the Literature." *PTSD Research Quarterly, National Center for PTSD* 9, no. 3 (2018).

Sharot, Tali, Elizabeth A. Martorella, Mauricio R. Delgado, and Elizabeth A. Phelps. "How Personal Experience Modulates the Neural Circuitry of Memories of September 11." *Proceedings of the National Academy of Sciences of the United States of America* 104, no. 1 (January 2, 2007): 389–94.

Smith, Emily Esfahani. "On Coronavirus Lockdown? Look for Meaning, Not Happiness." *New York Times*, April 7, 2020, sec. Opinion.

Solomon, Andrew. *The Noonday Demon: An Atlas of Depression.* New York: Scribner, 2001.

Southwick, Steven M., and Dennis S. Charney. *Resilience: The Science of Mastering Life's Greatest Challenges.* New York: Cambridge University Press, 2012.

Stefon, Matt. "Bardo Thödol | Tibetan Buddhist Text." Britannica, n.d. Web.

Stein, Michael. *The Lonely Patient: How We Experience Illness.* New York: Harper Perennial, 2008.

Tedeschi, Richard, and Lawrence Calhoun. "A Clinical Approach to Posttraumatic Growth." In *Positive Psychology in Practice,* 405–19, 2012.

Tippett, Krista. "Rachel Yehuda—How Trauma and Resilience Cross Generations." *On Being,* July 30, 2015. Podcast, 52:10.

Turnbull, Gordon. *Trauma: From Lockerbie to 7/7: How Trauma Affects Our Minds and How We Fight Back.* London: Bantam, 2011.

US Department of Veterans Affairs. "PTSD and Vietnam Veterans: A Lasting Issue 40 Years Later." June 22, 2016. Web.

van der Kolk, Bessel A. *The Body Keeps the Score: Brain, Mind, and Body in the Healing of Trauma.* New York: Viking, 2014.

Westphal, Maren, and George Bonanno. "Posttraumatic Growth and Resilience to Trauma: Different Sides of the Same Coin or Different Coins?" *Applied Psychology* 56, no. 3 (July 1, 2007): 417–27.

World Health Organization, International Classification of Diseases 11th Revision. "Mortality and Morbidity Statistics, Post Traumatic Stress Disorder." January 1, 2022. Web.

Yehuda, Rachel, and Joseph Ledoux. "Response Variation Following Trauma: A Translational Neuroscience Approach to Understanding PTSD." *Neuron* 56, no. 1 (November 1, 2007): 19–32.

Yehuda, R., and A. C. McFarlane. "Conflict Between Current Knowledge About Posttraumatic Stress Disorder and Its Original Conceptual Basis." *American Journal of Psychiatry* 152, no. 12 (December 1995): 1705–13.

12. PINS AND NEEDLES: PERIPHERAL NERVE REGENERATION

Altman, Lawrence K. "The Doctor's World; A Short, Speckled History of a Transplanted Hand." *New York Times*, February 27, 2001, sec. Science.

BBC World Service. "The World's First Hand Transplant." *Witness History*, September 23, 2014. Radio broadcast, 8:58.

Bhuvaneswar, Chaya G., Lucy A. Epstein, and Theodore A. Stern. "Reactions to Amputation: Recognition and Treatment." *Primary Care Companion to the Journal of Clinical Psychiatry* 9, no. 4 (February 2007): 303–8.

Bremner, Charles. "Pioneer Transplant Pair Share Their Ordeals." *The Times* (London), December 24, 2005. Infotrac Custom Newspapers.

Campbell, Fiona Kumari. "The Case of Clint Hallam's Wayward Hand: Print Media Representations of the 'Uncooperative' Disabled Patient." *Continuum* 18, no. 3 (September 1, 2004): 443–58.

CBC Radio. "Doctor Who Performed World's First Hand Transplant Recalls Complicated Surgery, Strange Aftermath." September 24, 2014. Radio broadcast, 8:15.

Datta, Dipak, Kanther Selvarajah, and Nicola Davey. "Functional Outcome of Patients with Proximal Upper Limb Deficiency–Acquired and Congenital." *Clinical Rehabilitation* 18, no. 2 (March 1, 2004): 172–77.

De Oliveira Chini, Gislaine Cristina, and Magali Roseira Boemer. "Amputation in the Perception of Those Who Experience It." *Revista Latino-Americana de Enfermagem* 15, no. 2 (April 2007): 330–36.

Dominion Post. "Hand-Transplant Man Ran Away with His Nurse." January 31, 2009.

Dubernard, Jean-Michel, Earl Owen, Nicole Lefrançois, Palmina Petruzzo, Xavier Martin, Marwan Dawahra, Denis Jullien, et al. "First Human Hand Transplantation." *Transplant International* 13, no. S1 (2000): S521–24.

Durkin, Joanne, Debra Jackson, and Kim Usher. "Touch in Times of COVID-19: Touch Hunger Hurts." *Journal of Clinical Nursing* 30, no. 1–2 (September 2021): e4–5.

Elbert, Thomas, Christo Pantev, Christian Wienbruch, Brigitte Rockstroh, and Edward Taub. "Increased Cortical Representation of the Fingers of the Left Hand in String Players." *Science* 270, no. 5234 (November 1, 1995): 305–7.

Frank, Michael. "An Exhibition Honors the Human Hand." *New York Times*, February 2, 2001.

Gaudet, Andrew D., Phillip G. Popovich, and Matt S. Ramer. "Wallerian Degeneration: Gaining Perspective on Inflammatory Events After Peripheral Nerve Injury." *Journal of Neuroinflammation* 8, no. 1 (August 30, 2011): 110.

Gesslbauer, Bernhard, Laura Hruby, Aidan Roche, Dario Farina, Roland Blumer, and Oskar Aszmann. "Axonal Components of Nerves Innervating the Human Arm." *Annals of Neurology* 82, no. 3 (August 18, 2017): 396–408.

Graczyk, Emily L., Linda Resnik, Matthew A. Schiefer, Melissa S. Schmitt, and Dustin J. Tyler. "Home Use of a Neural-Connected Sensory Prosthesis Provides the Functional and Psychosocial Experience of Having a Hand Again." *Scientific Reports* 8, no. 1 (June 29, 2018): 9866.

Bibliography

Grealish, A. "Loss, Challenge, Change: Psychological and Physical Aspects of Hand Injury." *The Lamp* 51, no. 7 (August 1994): 17–20.

Grob, M., N. A. Papadopulos, A. Zimmermann, E. Biemer, and L. Kovacs. "The Psychological Impact of Severe Hand Injury." *Journal of Hand Surgery (European Volume)* 33, no. 3 (June 1, 2008): 358–62.

Guardian. "Sleight of Hand." May 30, 2000.

Gustafsson, M., A. Amilon, and G. Ahlström. "Trauma-Related Distress and Mood Disorders in the Early Stage of an Acute Traumatic Hand Injury." *Journal of Hand Surgery (European Volume)* 28, no. 4 (August 2003): 332–38.

Hanna, Laurie. "UK's First Hand Transplant on the Way as Expert Unit Opens." *The Mirror*, December 27, 2011, sec. UK News.

Hasudungan, Armando. "Neurology - Nerve Damage and Regeneration." Armando Hasudungan Biology and Medicine Videos, 2014. YouTube video, 8:21.

Hunt, Tom. "Grasping at Straws with a Dead Man's Hand." *Dominion Post*, September 26, 2014.

Kumnig, Martin, Sheila G. Jowsey, Gerhard Rumpold, Annemarie Weissenbacher, Theresa Hautz, Timm O. Engelhardt, Gerald Brandacher, et al. "The Psychological Assessment of Candidates for Reconstructive Hand Transplantation." *Transplant International* 25, no. 5 (May 2012): 573–85.

McGinn, Colin. *Prehension: The Hand and the Emergence of Humanity*. Cambridge, MA: MIT Press, 2015.

MedlinePlus Genetics. "What Are Proteins and What Do They Do?" n.d. Web.

Menorca, Ron M. G., Theron S. Fussell, and John C. Elfar. "Peripheral Nerve Trauma: Mechanisms of Injury and Recovery." *Hand Clinics* 29, no. 3 (August 2013): 317–30.

Meyer, Therese M. "Psychological Aspects of Mutilating Hand Injuries." *Hand Clinics* 19, no. 1 (February 1, 2003): 41–49.

Mosley, Michael. "The Man Who's Had FOUR Hands: How Fire Victim Could Write Again After Amazing Limb Transplant." *Mail Online*, May 21, 2011, sec. Health.

Nathan, Adam, and Nayab Chohan. "Doctors Amputate First Transplanted Human Hand." *Sunday Times* (London), February 4, 2001. Infotrac Custom Newspapers.

Parkes, Colin Murray. "Psycho-Social Transitions: Comparison Between Reactions to Loss of a Limb and Loss of a Spouse." *British Journal of Psychiatry* 127, no. 3 (September 1975): 204–10.

Ray, Wilson Z., and Susan E. Mackinnon. "Management of Nerve Gaps: Autografts, Allografts, Nerve Transfers, and End-to-Side Neurorrhaphy." *Experimental Neurology* 223, no. 1 (May 2010): 77–85.

Rigoni, Michela, and Samuele Negro. "Signals Orchestrating Peripheral Nerve Repair." *Cells* 9, no. 8 (July 24, 2020): E1768.

Rybarczyk, Bruce, and Jay Behel. "Limb Loss and Body Image." In *Psychoprosthetics*, edited by Pamela Gallagher, Deirdre Desmond, and Malcolm MacLachlan, 23–31. London: Springer, 2008.

Sanger, James. "Early Psychological Aspects of Severe Hand Injury." *Journal of Hand Surgery: Journal of the British Society for Surgery of the Hand*, January 1, 1988.

Tennent, David, Joseph Wenke, Jessica Rivera, and Chad Krueger. "Characterisation and Outcomes of Upper Extremity Amputations." *Injury* 45, no. 6 (June 1, 2014): 965–69.

von Mohr, Mariana, Louise P. Kirsch, and Aikaterini Fotopoulou. "Social Touch Deprivation During COVID-19: Effects on Psychological Wellbeing and Craving Interpersonal Touch." *Royal Society Open Science* 8, no. 9 (n.d.): 210287.

Whelan, Lynsay R., and Jeremy Farley. "Functional Outcomes with Externally Powered Partial Hand Prostheses." *JPO: Journal of Prosthetics and Orthotics* 30, no. 2 (April 2018): 69–73.

Whittell, Giles. "'Remove My Hand.'" *The Times* (London), October 20, 2000.

World Health Organization, and The World Bank. "World Report on Disability." World Health Organization, 2011. Web.

Wysong, Pippa. "Advances in Hand and Face Transplantation: An Expert Interview with Dr. Jean-Michel Dubernard." Medscape Plastic Surgery, September 29, 2010. Web.

Zarrilli, Phillip B. "Where the Hand [Is] . . ." *Asian Theatre Journal* 4, no. 2 (Autumn 1987): 205–14.

14. IT'S ALL UP TO YOU, KIDDO: REHABILITATING A REPLANTED HAND

American Society for Surgery of the Hand. "About Hand Therapy." n.d. Web.

Cederlund, Ragnhikld, A. L. Thorén-Jönsson, and L. B. Dahlin. "Coping Strategies in Daily Occupations 3 Months After a Severe or Major Hand Injury." *Occupational Therapy International*, March 2010.

Eagleman, David. *Livewired: The Inside Story of the Ever-Changing Brain*. Edinburgh: Canongate Books, 2020.

Groth, Gail N. "Pyramid of Progressive Force Exercises to the Injured Flexor Tendon." *Journal of Hand Therapy* 17, no. 1 (January 1, 2004): 31–42.

Groth, G. N., and M. B. Wulf. "Compliance with Hand Rehabilitation: Health Beliefs and Strategies." *Journal of Hand Therapy* 8, no. 1 (March 1995): 18–22.

Hendren, Sara. *What Can a Body Do? How We Meet the Built World*. New York: Riverhead Books, 2020.

Kaskutas, Vicki, and Rhonda Powell. "The Impact of Flexor Tendon Rehabilitation Restrictions on Individuals' Independence with Daily Activities: Implications for Hand Therapists." *Journal of Hand Therapy* 26, no. 1 (January 1, 2013): 22–29.

Spicker, Paul. "Distinguishing Disability and Incapacity." *International Social Security Review* 56, no. 2 (July 14, 2003).

Sueoka, Stephanie Sato, and Paul C. LaStayo. "Zone II Flexor Tendon Rehabilitation: A Proposed Algorithm." *Journal of Hand Therapy* 21, no. 4 (October 1, 2008): 410–13.

Bibliography

Tang, Jin Bo, Peter C. Amadio, Martin I. Boyer, Robert Savage, Chunfeng Zhao, Michael Sandow, Steve K. Lee, and Scott W. Wolfe. "Current Practice of Primary Flexor Tendon Repair: A Global View." *Hand Clinics* 29, no. 2 (May 1, 2013): 179–89.

Yildirim, Azad, and Kemal Nas. "Evaluation of Postoperative Early Mobilization in Patients with Repaired Flexor Tendons of the Wrist, the Spaghetti Wrist." *Journal of Back and Musculoskeletal Rehabilitation* 23, no. 4 (November 5, 2010): 193–200.